)

Dartmoor's Earliest Photographs

Dartmoor's Earliest Photographs

Landscape & Place 1860-1880

by

Tom Greeves

TWELVEHEADS PRESS

TRURO 2015

For my friend, Chris Chapman,
a true master of Dartmoor photography

FRONT COVER: Gidleigh Church from east, with figures, c.1865. SX 671884. *Francis Bedford, no.1843.*

BACK COVER: Hunter's Tor from Whiddon Park, c.1865. SX 722897.
Francis Bedford, Devonshire Illustrated no.1852.

TWELVEHEADS PRESS

First published 2015 by Twelveheads Press
ISBN 978 0 906294 80 2
British Library Cataloguing-in-Publication Data.
A catalogue record for this book is available from the British Library.
Typeset in Garamond
Printed by Short Run Press Ltd, Exeter

CONTENTS

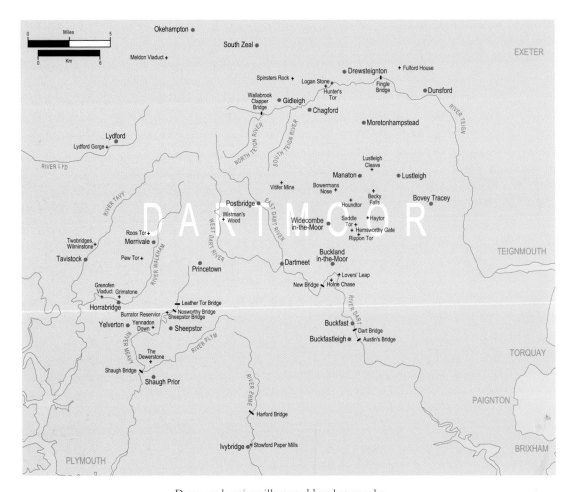

Dartmoor locations illustrated by photographs

LIST OF FIGURES

All are from the author's collection unless otherwise stated. The titles are modern descriptions and not necessarily the same as those on original photographs.

SV = Stereoview; **CDV** = Carte de Visite; **P** = photographic print.

ACKNOWLEDGEMENTS

The following people and institutions have helped me in various ways, and I am hugely indebted to them: John Anderson; Paul Anderton; Sadru Bhanji; Martin Bodman; Clare Broomfield, National Monuments Record; John Brown; Peter Brown; Chris Chapman; Cornwall Studies Library, Redruth; Geoff Cox; Marlene Creates; Devon & Exeter Institution; Kevin Dickens, Tavistock Museum; Gerry Falvey; Mary Green; Elisabeth Greeves; Bill and Judy Hardiman; Philip Kingslan John; Virginia Noonan; Stanley Oldfield; Nigel Overton, Plymouth City Museum; Godfrey Perkins; Plymouth Local Studies Library; Sue Price; Sylvia Sayer; Colin Smith, Bowdens, Chagford; Peter Stanier; Rob Steemson; Shelley Tobin; Martin Watts. Special thanks are due to Alan Kittridge of Twelveheads Press for his skilful design and editing.

Examples of
stereoview or
stereograph
cards (**SV**)

INTRODUCTION

The photographs in this book were taken when one of the best known of Dartmoor writers, William Crossing (1847-1928), was a teenager or a young man in his twenties, in the 1860s and 1870s. Through these images we can see the Dartmoor that inspired him, and which he and his contemporaries knew intimately. The photographs are the earliest record we have of the actual Dartmoor landscape, as opposed to artistic representations of it, and most of them (about ninety per cent) have never previously been published.

In 1983 I co-authored a book of photographs to celebrate the centenary of the Dartmoor Preservation Association.[1] I searched many sources for old photographs but at that time, apart from some images taken in 1873 on the occasion of the so-called military 'Autumn Manoeuvres', I knew of only a handful of views predating those by Robert Burnard (1848-1920), who seems to have begun documentary photography of Dartmoor in 1887.[2] I was very wary of assigning a date before 1880 to any image. Even when I published a book of Dartmoor photographs in 2004[3] I was hesitant to assign early dates, and that of Nosworthy Bridge[4] which I gave then as c. 1890 is assuredly nearer 1865 (**105**), and that of South Zeal (**128**)[5] which I suggested belonged to the 1880s is, I now think, probably two decades earlier. Such is the pleasure and progress of research!

Charles Thomas's scholarly publication *Views and Likenesses* in 1988[6] opened eyes to potential photographic riches of earlier decades, but still Dartmoor images were not forthcoming. In 1999 my wife gave me a stereoview, acquired by her some years before, which I realised was a very early image of Postbridge (**3**) and this changed everything. It also coincided with the arrival of the internet and Ebay auctions which have enabled sellers to present images which would otherwise never have seen the light of day. I have searched and enquired of photographic archives but, with a handful of exceptions, few have 'early' images (i.e. pre-1880). I am very grateful for the help of several local collectors and dealers (especially Sadru Bhanji, Geoff Cox, Gerald Quinn and Robert Sampson).

Recent publications such as those on J. W. G. Gutch[7] and Francis

Bedford[8] have further stimulated interest in early photography in the south-west of England.

I now realise that there are probably several hundred extant Dartmoor photographs of these two decades (1860s and 1870s) and many of them are yet to be revealed. I present here what I consider to be the most interesting and finest quality of those that I am aware of now. This is a book essentially about the Dartmoor landscape of the mid-nineteenth century so I have omitted early portraiture of individuals, some of which will definitely date to the 1850s. However, people do feature in a significant number of the images here. Not only are these the earliest photographic images of people within a Dartmoor context, but they also provide a fascinating glimpse into costume and, occasionally, working conditions of the 1860s and 1870s (e.g. 13 and 115).

The date range must be considered somewhat fluid – without a contemporary dated subject or ownership inscription, a date tied to a year can be difficult to give. That several of the images date to the late 1850s is almost certain, but it would seem wise to put a starting date of about 1860. We can be confident, for example, that Spreat's images will mostly predate 1865, that Bedford's probably fall mostly within the range of 1865-1875, that Merrifield's and those of Way & Sons probably date mostly from the late 1850s to the mid-1860s. A cautious approach will tend to give a slightly more recent date than perhaps the photographs deserve, but ongoing 'detective' work will refine dates as time passes.

Clothing is an indicator of date, allowing perhaps for conservatism among Dartmoor people – Samuel Rowe comments in some detail on the old-fashioned styles of dress in use in the Chagford area in the 1840s.[9] People photographed include the middle classes (e.g. Chagford church choir (43), Parlby wedding (74), picnickers (96)) but also country 'yeomen' (e.g. Spinsters' Rock (33); Gidleigh (34)) and labourers (Vitifer Mine (13); Fitzford Gatehouse (115)).

In 1852 J. G. Croker advised any moorland traveller that they needed 'a fear-nought carriage and horse and good personal pluck' for their Dartmoor expeditions [10], but by the 1860s railways were making access easier. Yet one still has to admire the resourcefulness of the photographers in reaching the subjects they wanted to capture, with their precious glass plate negatives, chemicals, water, valuable cameras and portable darkrooms. In 1867 Francis Bedford published a paper titled 'Landscape Photography and its Trials' in which he cited wind as the greatest enemy, and the need for the photographer to have 'wonderful patience and determined devotion to his art'.[11] As early as 1861 he himself had invented 'a travelling carriage, functioning as transport, sleeping accommodation, and darkroom'.[12]

After initial developments in photography in the 1820s and 1830s especially by Louis Daguerre, and then by William Henry Fox Talbot in the 1840s, photographic establishments began to proliferate in the 1850s. There had been a surge of interest in stereoscopic photography following the Great Exhibition of 1851 and endorsement by Queen Victoria and Prince Albert. Stereoviews (otherwise known as stereographs) became immensely popular in the 1860s and 1870s when millions were produced. Two almost identical and approximately square photographic prints were stuck closely side-by-side on long cards which commonly range in size from 172 x 83 mm (6.8 x 3.3 inches) to 178 x 85 mm (7.0 x 3.4 inches). Most are on yellow card but others are on white card, which are thought to be earliest in date. A few (Stereoscopic Gems) are on green card. When viewed through a stereoscope, a single image appears, miraculously, as if in three dimensions. Cartes-de-visite, promoted by Andre Disdéri from 1854, were also very popular, especially in the 1860s. They were printed on white card commonly ranging in size from 102 x 64 mm to 104 x 63 mm (4.0 x 2.5 inches). Both stereoviews and cartes-de-visite sold for about one shilling each.

To appreciate the extraordinary impact that photography must have had it is useful to compare early nineteenth century engravings of many of the scenes which were photographed by these pioneers.[13] Lovely as the engraved images are in artistic terms, they are not necessarily renowned for their accuracy in depicting landscape. With photography there was no doubt – this is what you saw when there and, by using a stereoscope giving a three-dimensional image, you could feel part of the very place shown.

Carte-de-visite
(CDV)
approximately
actual size

1. Postbridge from SW, August 1889. SX 648788. *Robert Burnard*. **P**

CENTRAL DARTMOOR

THE ARCHAEOLOGY OF PHOTOGRAPHY (POSTBRIDGE)

The remarkable age of some photographic images of the Dartmoor landscape is demonstrated well by these three views of Postbridge. The first (1) was taken by Robert Burnard in 1889 looking over the ruins of a building towards the famous clapper bridge over the East Dart river. The second (2) was taken by a Totnes photographer, J. Brinley, in about 1875. We can be confident of this because one of the stones from the central portion of the bridge is seen lying in the river and it is known that this was replaced in 1879.[14] Brinley's photograph shows, in the background, the same ruins as in Burnard's image, but much better preserved. The third and earliest

2. Postbridge, looking SW, c. 1875 SX 648788. *J. Brinley, Totnes.* **P.** (detail above)

3. Postbridge,
looking SW, early
1860s. SX 648788.
*William Spreat, 229
High Street, Exeter
no. 304.* **SV**
(detail below)

photograph (3), on a stereoview card published by William Spreat of Exeter, probably dates to around 1860 – remarkably, it shows the building in the background, roofed and occupied, with smoke coming out of its chimney. This, as it happens, was the first Dartmoor stereoview of which I became aware, given to me by my wife Elisabeth in 1999. It spurred me on to seek out others.

The building in question was known as 'The Barracks' and was the last survivor of a complex constructed in 1786 by William Warren and which included a tin smelting house.[15] All that survives now are some very indistinct walls and a fine tin mouldstone.

DARTMEET

Dartmeet has long been a popular destination but these early images show a marked contrast to the present day, when much of the river and its immediate surroundings are obscured by trees compared to the open landscape of 150 years ago – an observation that can be made of many of the images.

William Spreat took several photographs of the Dartmeet area. A very interesting scene (4) shows the area of the modern carpark and the site of the present Badger's Holt cafe, upstream of the bridge. It shows the cottages which once existed here, lived in by the Leaman family in the second half of the nineteenth century. A Joey Leaman who lived here in the later nineteenth century, and who had been injured in an accident at Powder Mills, near Postbridge, used to be teased by boys who would cover the chimney of his cottage and shout 'Smoke the badger out! Smoke the badger out!' This is the origin of the name of the tearooms.[16] Another luminous view

4. River Dart above Dartmeet, early 1860s. SX 672733. *William Spreat, 229 High Street, Exeter.* **SV** (detail above)

5. Dartmeet Bridge and confluence of East and West Dart - view down Dartmeet Hill, early 1860s. SX 672733. *William Spreat, 229 High Street, Exeter.* **SV**

(5) by Spreat shows the lower part of Dartmeet Hill, the bridge, and the view up the West Dart, including rough ground of Combestone farm, across the river in Holne parish.

Published as a carte-de-visite by Francis Bedford is a view (6) looking up the West Dart, but also showing its confluence with the East Dart. Land belonging to Combestone farm is seen on the left.

A. L. Coke of Newton Abbot produced a fine image (7) of Dartmeet Bridge from the downstream side. The bridge had been built in 1792 by William Taylor of Bickington at a cost of £195.[17] The cottage partly

6. Dartmeet –
confluence of East
and West Dart,
c. 1870.
SX 672731.
*Francis Bedford,
no.2026.* **CDV**

7. Dartmeet Bridge
from downstream,
c. 1870.
SX 672732.
*Archibald L. Coke,
Newton Abbot,
no.255.* **SV**
(E. Greeves collection)

8. Dartmeet –
cottage on west
side of bridge
(detail), c. 1870.
SX 672732.
Francis Bedford,
Devonshire
Illustrated no.2025.
SV

visible on the left is shown in a detail (**8**) from a stereoview by Bedford, revealing it to be thatched. An inscription on a carte-de-visite (**9**) by Spreat records that the cottage was occupied at the time by a Mrs Caunter. Part of the cottage is shown, with a small van and figure on the bridge itself. This may well be the photographer's van containing equipment.

9. Dartmeet Bridge and Dartmeet Hill, early 1860s. SX 672732. *William Spreat, 229 High Street, Exeter no. 571.* **CDV** (E. Greeves collection)

WISTMAN'S WOOD

About five miles north-west of Dartmeet is Wistman's Wood, dominated
by contorted pedunculate oak (*Quercus robur*) trees, thought to be relicts of
Dartmoor's post-Ice Age vegetation, and considered a remarkable
phenomenon since at least the early seventeenth century when noted by
Thomas Risdon.[18] This view (**10**) by Spreat, previously published by
Bhanji,[19] is the earliest known photographic depiction of it, and of great
interest ecologically, as the wood has fluctuated in size through time. The
view is taken in summer from the west side of the West Dart river,
looking to Longaford Tor on the horizon. This was probably some twenty
years before a fire in 1886 destroyed part of the wood,[20] and it shows
Middle Wood which appears slightly more extensive than its state in
about 1900,[21] but much reduced compared to its modern condition.

PRINCETOWN PRISON

Of special interest and importance is this view (**11**) of the prison at Princetown in about 1860. It shows it before radical rebuilding of the cell blocks between 1880-1913 (including the addition of the present-day iconic massive chimneys) on the same radial layout as the original buildings.[22] It is the earliest known photograph of the prison, and was almost certainly taken by William Merrifield of Tavistock. F. C. Lewis published a print (**12**) of the Napoleonic war prison (built 1806-1809) in 1821[23] which shows how relatively little it had changed since then. The photograph was taken a decade after conversion to a convict prison and conveys well the impression of the original war prison, despite some additions such as the administration block with a clocktower in the centre, presumably built in or soon after 1850. The view looks north-eastwards from the lower slopes of Hessary Tor to Bellever Tor and Laughter Tor on the horizon. The road to Two Bridges can be seen on the right. The famous prison gate is clearly seen.

11. Convict Prison, Princetown
c. 1860.
SX 586741.
William Merrifield, Tavistock. **SV**
(glass negative, Merrifield Collection, Tavistock Museum)

12. War Prison, Princetown, 1821.
SX 586741.
Engraving in
F. C. Lewis (1821)

VITIFER MINE

Just under three miles north-east of Postbridge below the Warren House Inn was Vitifer Mine – the largest and most important moorland tin mine of the eighteenth and nineteenth centuries

This photograph (13) is perhaps the most remarkable and unexpected image to come to light in preparation of this book. I was sent a copy of it electronically by a friend and colleague (a specialist on mills), who wondered if I could identify its location. Almost immediately I knew exactly what scene it depicted. Anxious to track down the original, I learnt that my friend had been sent it by a colleague in Dorset who had himself been sent it by the chairman of that county's industrial archaeology society. The latter had been sent it by his historian brother in Staffordshire, who had been shown the original by its owner from Cheshire! Emails and correspondence through another party eventually produced a result and a fine copy image.

The photograph dates to the early 1860s and shows a group of sixteen Dartmoor tin miners (men and boys) at Vitifer Mine, posed beside a large cast iron waterwheel. The background view is of the Redwater valley looking towards Challacombe Down. In the middle distance on the left are sheds which are precursors of the later main Vitifer Mine dressing floor.[24] Everywhere in the valley itself is bare ground turned over by the tinners. This was the peak period of Birch Tor & Vitifer Mine - 150 persons were employed above and below ground in 1863.[25]

The photograph is around twenty-five years earlier than any previously known image of mining machinery on moorland Dartmoor (Burnard's view of a waterwheel at Whiteworks in 1889 – see Greeves, 1986, Plate 2) and about forty years earlier than any previously confirmed image of miners themselves (Chapman & Son postcards of miners at Vitifer and Golden Dagger in the early years of the twentieth century - Greeves, 1986, passim). It is also the first known photograph of this particular waterwheel.

The location can be precisely identified at SX 68178090. The heap of spoil on which the group is positioned, and the heap in the foreground, both still exist in exactly this form. The stone-lined pit for the waterwheel is still visible and measures internally 13m x 1.5m (43ft x 5ft).[26] The wheel appears to have been used for pumping Dunstan's Shaft – named after Capt. Richard Dunstan, this was being sunk in 1848 and eventually reached a depth of at least 40 fathoms (240ft)[27] – but was probably also used for stamping (i.e. crushing) ore. The photograph confirms neither of these functions, and it may be that the wheel was newly installed and still had additions to be made, or was being refurbished.

It is exceptional for a photograph of this era to show a posed group of working people. No other 'group' photograph taken by Spreat is yet

known. Two underground miners are distinctly shown – 4th and 5th from the left in the front row are men with underground clothes and hard hats each with a lump of clay and a candle stuck on it. The righthand man has tallow candles slung round his neck. A third, younger, man, second from right in the front row, is also wearing underground clothes and is holding his hat. He appears to be wearing a close-fitting skullcap. The attire of these underground miners looks very similar to that of fifty years later in the early 1900s. The remaining adult men and boys look distinctly more 'old-fashioned' in their dress, with braces holding up their trousers which appear to have a front flap, and waistcoats.

13. Vitifer Tin Mine, miners by waterwheel at Dunstans Shaft, early 1860s. SX 682809. *William Spreat, 4 Gandy Street, Exeter.* SV (J. Anderson collection)

14. Logan Stone, River Teign, c. 1865. SX 723898. *Anonymous.* **SV**

A CLOCKWISE CIRCUIT OF DARTMOOR
FROM ITS NORTH-EASTERN EDGE

THE LOGAN STONE

Every visitor to Dartmoor from the mid-eighteenth century until at least the end of the nineteenth century would have considered visiting the massive boulder on the left bank of the Teign which was said to rock by the touch of a human hand. Such rocks were thought to be poised and venerated by the Druids and so have a sacred purpose. But fashions change, and this rock is now obscured and neglected. However, its previous high status is well documented.

The site of the boulder is shown on Benjamin Donn's map of Devon which was published in 1765 after some five summers of fieldwork completed in 1763.[28] It is marked (on Sheet 6b) as 'Moving Rock'.

The Revd John Swete's manuscript journal records a visit to the 'Moving Rock' in September 1789[29]: '... a stupendous block of Granate detached, and resting at its base on a rising narrow point of another mass, deep-grounded in the channel of the river an equipoise was thus wonderfully formed – which tho' by accounts given in the neighbourhood was not so sensible as it had been in former times, was yet to be put in motion by pressing with some force against it...The Dimensions of this stone are enormous! at the west end it is ten feet high and from the West to the Eastern point the length may be about 18 feet.' A painting of it is dated October 1792.[30]

Richard Polwhele published a description and discussion of it in 1793,[31] using remarkably similar language to that of Swete, with whom he often travelled on excursions: 'The *Moving-rock* is thus poised upon another mass of stone, which is deep-grounded in the bed of the river: it is unequally sided, of great size, at some parts six, at others seven feet in height, and at the west end, ten. From its west to its east points, it may be in length about eighteen feet. It is flattish on the top. It seems to touch the stone below in three or four places; but, probably, it is the gravel which the floods have left between, that causes this appearance. I easily rocked it with one hand, but its quantity of motion did not exceed one inch, if so much. The equipoise, however, was more perceptible a few years since: and it was, probably, balanced with such nicety in former times, as to move with the slightest touch. It is remarkable, that the surface of the lower stone is somewhat sloping, so that it should seem easy to shove off the upper stone; but the united efforts of a number of men, who endeavoured to displace it, had not the smallest effect.' He surmises that, although the rock is obviously natural, it 'must have been an admirable engine of priestcraft, and have operated on the multitude precisely as the Druids wished'.[32]

In 1796 a description and illustration of the logan stone was published by 'N.E.'[Revd John Swete]. He wrote, '...the country people ...call it a Logging-stone, a stupendous block of granite, detached and resting at its base on a rising narrow point of another mass, deep-grounded in the channel of the river Teign. An equipoise was thus formed, and though by accounts given in the neighbourhood, the motion had ceased to be so sensible, as in former times, it was yet to be produced by pressing against the stone with some force...The dimensions of this stone are enormous; at the west end it is ten feet high, and from the west to the eastern point, the length may be about eighteen feet. The local circumstances of it are almost as extraordinary as the stone itself. The river Teign rolls its waters around, and it is seated among those wild romantic hills, whose shaggy sides are overspread with fragments separated from the crags above – on the bold tufted crest of the opposite eminence, in Widdon park, groups of deer are seen, during the mid day heats of summer, inhaling the breezes of the hills, and silence would have kept a repose uninterrupted, had it not been broken by the crash of the shattered rocks or the shrill cry of the mountain kite'.[33]

The Revd Richard Warner of Bath visited the stone in September 1799 and found it had no 'oscillatory motion'. He was guided by a diminutive but sprightly tailor from Chagford who 'skipped on with the alertness of a flea' and who 'insisted that five and thirty years ago [i.e. 1764] it might have been moved by a child'.[34]

In September 1828 Samuel Rowe noted 'On the application of considerable strength at its east end, its motion is just perceptible'.[35] In his *Perambulation of the... Forest of Dartmoor*[36] he gives a precise description of the rock: 'It is an irregular pentagonal mass, the sides of which are of the following dimensions. Eastern, five feet four inches in width; northern, seven feet eight; north-west, six feet four; south-east five feet four; and the southern, towards the river, ten feet six. It is about seven feet and a half in height at the western corner. This huge mass rests on a single rock and still *loggs* perceptibly, but very slightly, by the application of one man's strength...'

On 15 August 1856 some gentlemen and ladies had a picnic under a tree in Whiddon Park. A journal records: 'Visited the Logan Stone, the Ladies scaling the Park wall manfully, and crossing the river on a Ladder

15. Logan Stone,
River Teign,
c. 1865.
SX 723898.
*Francis Bedford,
Devonshire
Illustrated no. 1825.*
SV

like witches on a Broom Stick. Mr H and I moved it slightly by the
application of our shoulders; but he says that it may be moved to a greater
extent by two persons getting on the top, and jumping on the end'.[37]

Black's *Guide to Devonshire* of 1864 [38] noted of the stone that 'many a
legend flourished about it in the days of our childhood; but even
Devonshire peasants have tasted of the fruit of "the tree of knowledge,"
and now regard the Logan Stone with a sublime indifference.'

An anonymous stereo photograph (14), with a person lying on a
nearby rock, shows its context in the river well. A closer view (15) is by
Bedford. A third image (16) is an amusing close-up view showing a
horizontal figure of a man face-down and resting his head on his hands,
seemingly about to be crushed by the rock. This has a printed label which
suggests that it is almost certainly by Way & Sons of Torquay and which
may therefore date to the late 1850s or very early 1860s. The latter image
seems to have been the source of an engraving (17) (without the human
figure) used by Philip Henry Gosse in 1865 at the start of the section on
'Dartmoor and the Dart' in his book *Sea and Land*.[39] He may well have
acquired the photograph when staying at St Marychurch.

16. Logan Stone,
River Teign, with
figure, c. 1860.
SX 723898.
Anonymous but
probably *Way &
Sons, Torquay.* **SV**

BELOW:
17. Logan Stone,
River Teign, early
1860s. SX 723898.
Engraving in *P.
Gosse* (1865)

BELOW RIGHT:
18. Logan Stone,
River Teign,
modern view.
SX 723898.
T. Greeves.
Digital image

LOGAN STONE, NEAR CHAGFORD.

19. River Teign, view upstream to Hunter's Tor from Piddledown, early 1860s. SX 727900 (viewpoint). *William Spreat, 229 High Street, Exeter no.245.* **SV**

20. River Teign, view upstream to Hunter's Tor from Piddledown, modern view. SX 727900 (viewpoint). *T. Greeves.* Digital image

A contemporary photograph (18) shows the appearance of the stone today, at SX 723898, neglected and unvisited, despite being marked on Ordnance Survey maps well into the twentieth century at SX 723898 (e.g. OS Sheet 78.14, 2nd edn 1905).

The wider context of this location is seen in this photograph (19) by Spreat, taken from Piddledown Crags, looking upstream to Hunter's Tor and on towards Chagford. The logan stone is just visible halfway up the river on the righthand side. Juxtaposed is a modern view (20) of this scene,

showing how woodland now dominates this valley. The contrast between wooded Whiddon Park and rough scrubland on the north side of the river was much admired by writers of the eighteenth and early nineteenth centuries.

A short distance upstream of the famous logan stone is Hunter's Tor otherwise Hunt's Tor, seen in this superb image (**21**) by Bedford, taken from Whiddon Park. A magnificent ridge of rock is seen running from the riverside up to a plateau where, fifty years later (in the early twentieth century), Castle Drogo was to be built. Nowadays this view is shrouded in woodland.

21. Hunter's Tor from Whiddon Park, c. 1865. SX 722897. *Francis Bedford, Devonshire Illustrated no. 1852.* **SV**

FINGLE BRIDGE AND RIVER TEIGN

The ancient bridge and the picturesque mill a short distance downstream from it, set within the spectacular scenery of the Teign gorge, attracted visitors from the eighteenth century onwards. Black's *Guide*[40] of 1864 said 'no tourist should fail to visit' Fingle Bridge.

The striking photograph (22) by Bedford encapsulates the beauty of the bridge. A view (23), probably

22. Fingle Bridge, River Teign, from downstream side, c. 1865.
SX 743899.
Francis Bedford, Devonshire Illustrated no. 1820.
SV
(detail opposite)

23. Fingle Bridge,
River Teign, from
upstream side,
c. 1860.
SX 743899.
Anonymous, but
probably *Way &
Sons, Torquay.* **SV**

by Way & Sons of Torquay, shows a figure lying on rocks in the middle of the river, and looks downstream to the bridge and the steep slope of Prestonbury on the left. Two stereoviews (**24** and **25**), both by Spreat, look upstream to the bridge and beyond, and reveal active management of the woodland on the Drewsteignton side of the valley. One (**24**) has an ownership ink inscription on the back with the date 'Nov 7th 1865'. This was a time of charcoal production and also bark collection (for tanning).

24. Fingle Bridge,
River Teign,
looking upstream,
early 1860s.
SX 743899.
William Spreat, 229
High Street, Exeter
no.243. **SV**

25. Fingle Bridge,
River Teign,
looking upstream,
early 1860s.
SX 743899.
William Spreat, 229
High Street, Exeter
no.521. **SV**

26. Fingle Bridge, River Teign, looking downstream from the bridge, early 1860s. SX 743899. *William Spreat, 229 High Street, Exeter no.523.* **SV**

Another Spreat view (**26**) looks downstream from the bridge, showing the flat meadow (devoid of trees) on the right bank, close to the mill, with the precipitous slope of Prestonbury on the left. Bedford's image (**27**) of a fisherman was taken just upstream of the bridge.

27. Fingle Bridge, River Teign with fisherman, looking upstream, c. 1865. SX 743899. *Francis Bedford , Devonshire Illustrated no. 1823.* **SV** (detail below)

Fingle Mill was the only source of refreshment for visitors before Jessie Ashplant began selling teas by the bridge in 1897 and then opened a roofed tea room in 1907 on the site of what was to become the Anglers' Rest.[41] In Black's *Guide to Devonshire* (1864) it was noted of the mill that 'a couple of rooms are placed at the disposal of visitors'. Murray's *A Handbook for Travellers in Devon & Cornwall* (1872)[42] notes 'A mill is prettily situated a short distance below the bridge, and the miller, who gravely offends by diverting the water from the bed of the stream, provides, in deprecation of the traveller's resentment, a parlour and kitchen, with which parties bringing their own provisions are accommodated'. It was an ancient corn mill, listed in a survey of 1639/40 as being in possession of the Courtenay family[43], and may have also been an iron mill at one time (iron slag has been found by the author on the site). The photograph (**28**), perhaps dating

28. Fingle Mill,
River Teign,
c.1880.
SX 744897.
*Stereoscopic Gems,
English Scenery.* SV

29. Artist by leat
to Fingle Mill,
River Teign,
c. 1880.
SX 744897.
Stereoscopic Gems,
English Scenery. SV

30. On the Teign,
near Chagford,
c. 1860.
Exact location
unknown.
Way & Sons'
Stereoscopic
Illustrations of
Devonshire Scenery.
SV
(detail bottom
right)

from about 1880, shows clearly an unusual undershot waterwheel. A record of 31 December 1926, by which time the mill had been long abandoned, noted that there had previously been two wheels in operation, probably in tandem, each 11ft 9 ins in diameter x 1ft 7 ins breast.[44] The Brely family were millers at Fingle for several generations from at least the late eightenth century. In July 1894 the corn mill burnt down, when the Parr family were in occupation.[45]

Another image of about 1880 (**29**) shows an artist at work, by the leat leading to the mill wheel. The ruins of the mill are still visible and accessible today.

Way & Sons produced an amusing stereo photograph (**30**) of a disconsolate fisherman sitting on a tree-trunk in the dried-up river bed of the River Teign, against a colossal boulder, and holding a less than adequate rod.

On the moorland Wallabrook, by its junction with the North Teign, is this earliest known photographic record (**31**) of the single clapper bridge here, by T. Brinley of Totnes. The straightened and walled channel of the river was created by medieval tinners in order to speed up flow and to drain miry ground upstream, so that they could exploit rich alluvial tin deposits.

31. Wallabrook clapper bridge, looking upstream, c. 1875.
SX 654871.
T. Brinley, Totnes.
CDV

SPINSTERS' ROCK

Equal to the Logan Stone as a desirable destination for eighteenth and
nineteenth century travellers was the relatively nearby 'cromlech'
known as Spinsters' Rock, between Drewsteignton and Chagford. It is
the stone framework of a prehistoric chambered tomb with a massive
capstone resting on three supports. It attracted the attention of
antiquaries from at least the mid-eighteenth century, and is described
and discussed by Chapple in 1779, and by Polwhele in 1793, who
devoted some thirty pages of close text to it.[46] It was illustrated in
engravings by John Swete in 1796[47] and by Samuel Lysons, from the
east, in 1807.[48]

In the early 1860s and maybe even earlier, a solicitor, George Wareing
Ormerod (1810-1891) who lived near Chagford, was among pioneers
taking photographs in the locality. As early as July 1855 he recorded the
cromlech in detail by means of the Camera Lucida technique,[49] whereby a
mirror reflects an image of the scene or object onto a drawing surface.
Three of his drawings labelled 'From South', 'From North West' and

'From North' were reproduced in 1872 though, more accurately, their viewpoints are from SE, W and NNW respectively. On 27 January 1862 he attempted a photograph of Spinsters' Rock but poor light prevented success. Four days later the structure collapsed, and he photographed it in this state on 21 February 1862. Although an engraving from this photograph was reproduced in 1872, his original negative or print has not yet been found. A remarkable restoration, completed on 7 November 1862, was carried out by John Ball (recorded as Thomas Ball in Ormerod, 1871, 411) and William Stone of Chagford. To give stability to the structure the easternmost of the supporting orthostats was turned through ninety degrees.[50] Ormerod photographed the process and end result[51] but his prints have not been traced. Hopefully, pre-restoration photographs may yet come to light.

A stereoview (**32**) by Spreat is from the SSW and was probably taken not long after the restoration. Interestingly, it appears to show a ring bank of lighter soil surrounding the structure, which may be a genuine prehistoric element. A good view (**33**) by Bedford, published as a carte-de-visite, perhaps of about 1865, is taken from the west. The seated figure may be that of a local farmer. The buildings of Shilstone are seen behind.

33. The Spinsters' Rock chambered tomb, near Drewsteignton, from west, c. 1865. SX 701908. *Francis Bedford, no. 1827.* **CDV**

43

34. Gidleigh
Church from east,
with figures,
c.1865.
SX 671884.
*Francis Bedford,
no.1843.* **CDV**

GIDLEIGH

The tiny community of Gidleigh on north-east Dartmoor is a separate
parish. This carte-de-visite (**34**) by Bedford is unusual for the relatively
close view of people in the foreground. The two young men on the
righthand side may well be Bedford's two sons, Arthur (1845-1867) and
William (b.1846).[52] They are dressed in typical middleclass clothes of the

35. Gidleigh Castle
from south, c.1870.
SX 671885.
Frith's Carte Series.
CDV

period. The man and boy standing in the middle of the road look as if they are local people and have clothing of a 'lower' class status. In the background is Gidleigh church with the roof of its porch thickly covered in ivy.

A fine record of the medieval fortified manor house known as Gidleigh Castle is seen in this view (35) by Frith, dating to around 1870. The clear detail of the stonework is an important record of the building which, although recently lovingly restored, has lost some of its stonework in the past 150 years. On the right of the picture are buildings which no longer exist.

CHAGFORD

Chagford has been an important centre for centuries. The photograph (36) taken from Meldon Hill by James Valentine, perhaps in about 1880, captures its setting well. But Spreat's view from the south-east (37), which probably dates to the early 1860s, gives a better impression of the

36. Chagford from Meldon Hill, c.1880. SX 701875. *James Valentine* 7703. **P**

37. Chagford from the south-east, c.1865.
SX 701875.
William Spreat, 4 Gandy Street, Exeter, no.574. **SV**
(detail below)

medieval stannary town with its long thatched buildings and the ancient church tower on the right. The allotments in the middle distance are now the site of the Jubilee Hall and carpark. The walled garden is attached to the old rectory, now known as Chagford House, formerly the residence of the Hayter-Hames family.[53]

Francis Bedford took this fine photograph (38) of the deeply cut lane leading down to Chagford Bridge in about 1865. The two men are very probably his sons Arthur and William. In the middle distance a very large building is visible – this is the woollen mill at Factory Cross established by Mr Berry in 1800 and a major source of employment for weavers. It closed in 1848 but reopened for a time until about 1880, but is now completely ruined.[54]

Fortunately some even earlier views of Chagford survive, dating to about 1860 or the late 1850s. The photographer is unknown and the original negatives and prints have not been traced, but they may well have been taken by local solicitor G. W. Ormerod who took images of

40. The Square,
Chagford, c. 1860.
SX 701875.
Anonymous,
but possibly
G. W. Ormerod. **P**
(copy in Sue Price
collection)

Spinsters' Rock (see above). He is known to have taken other photographs of the Chagford area at this time – William Crossing says he photographed a stone with an incised cross below Cranbrook Castle in 1863 [55] and his record of the Chagford Archery Society in 1863 has been published.[56] Two photographs (39 and 40) show Chagford Square and the old thatched market house known as 'The Shambles', which was demolished in July 1862.[57] Two views (41 and 42) are of Mill Street at the same period. MURCH and MORRISH are visible above doorways, and also a hanging sign of the Baker's Arms.

41. Mill Street
from The Square,
Chagford, c.1860.
SX 700875.
Anonymous,
but possibly
G. W. Ormerod. **P**
(copy in Sue Price
collection)

A splendid record of Chagford Church Choir is this damaged print (43) of a photograph taken in 1865.

Holy Street Mill, less than a mile from the centre of Chagford, was a much-favoured spot for artists and visitors. A highly picturesque ancient and thatched corn mill was irresistible. A photograph by Frith in about

42. Mill Street, Chagford, looking towards the parish church, c. 1860. SX 700875. *Anonymous,* but possibly *G. W. Ormerod*. **P** (copy in Sue Price collection)

43. Chagford Church Choir, 1865. *Anonymous,* but possibly *G. W. Ormerod*. **P** (Smith collection, Bowdens)

44. Holy Street
Mill, near
Chagford, from the
north, c.1870.
SX 689879.
Frith's Carte Series
no.5776. **CDV**

1870 (44) sets the romantic scene admirably. The view is looking south towards the mill, and beyond to Meldon Hill. An umbrella on the left shades an artist at his easel. A fine study of the mill (45), also by Frith, shows the whole mill building and the waterwheel of about 14ft diameter on its north side. A superb detail of the mill wheel (46), capturing the wetness on the iron axle and the wooden supporting timbers, was published in the series titled 'Stereoscopic Gems'. The printed label on

45. Holy Street
Mill, near
Chagford, c.1870.
SX 689879.
Frith's Carte Series
no. 5774. **CDV**

46. Holy Street
Mill, near
Chagford, c. 1880.
SX 689879.
*Stereoscopic Gems,
English Scenery.* **SV**

the back noted that in the summer the mill was 'infested with artists' and mentioned that the late Thomas Creswick R.A. (1811-1869) had painted it three times. A stereoview (47) by A. L. Coke of Newton Abbot, labelled 'Holy Street Mill, Chagford', shows a waterwheel on the south side of the building, which is not otherwise recorded except in a lithograph of 1844 by William Spreat.[58] There is good detail of the covered cart in the foreground. Spreat recorded

47. Holy Street Mill, near Chagford, showing waterwheel on south side, c.1865. SX 689879. *Archibald L. Coke, Devonshire Scenery.* **SV**

48. Holy Street
Bridge, River
Teign, c.1865.
SX 689878.
William Spreat,
229 High Street,
Exeter, no.528. **SV**

the footbridge (**48**) with a very sturdy wooden fence, which led to the mill across the South Teign river. Two figures are just visible on the bridge.

Dunsford

Dunsford parish church of St Mary is shown in this stereoview (**49**) by Owen Angel of Exeter who described himself on the printed label as a 'Photographist'. Within this parish on the eastern edge of Dartmoor is Fulford House, photographed (**50**) by Spreat. The Fulford family have lived here for centuries and have often been very closely linked to Dartmoor. For example, Sir Thomas Fulford of the late fifteenth century was much involved with tinworks, being several times accused of malpractice.[59]

49. Dunsford
Church, c. 1865.
SX 813893.
Owen Angel, Exeter.
SV

50. Fulford House,
Dunsford, c.1865.
SX 791917.
William Spreat,
4 Gandy Street,
Exeter, no.366. **SV**

51. Fore Street, Moretonhampstead, c. 1865. SX 754861. *Francis Bedford, Devonshire Illustrated no. 1808.* **SV**

MORETONHAMPSTEAD

Fore Street, Moretonhampstead, is shown in this superb view (51) by Francis Bedford, looking towards the church. The definition of the cobbles is specially fine. A man, probably one of Bedford's sons, is talking to three working women, one of whom wears a 'pork pie' hat; the other two are standing in their doorways with their hooped crinoline dresses billowing out. A man on the right stands in a doorway above which is a sign reading SEARLE. He is very probably 'boot and shoemaker' Henry Searle who is listed in directories as being in Fore Street in 1866[60] and 1873. He was still there in 1878 when he was described as 'shoemaker, emigration agent'.[61] The buildings on the left are now much altered. The church of St Andrew is shown in this well composed view (52) by Bedford.

52.
Moretonhampstead Church from the south-east, c.1865. SX 755861.
Francis Bedford, Devonshire Illustrated no. 1809.
SV

53. Cross Tree,
Moretonhampstead,
c.1865.
SX 755860.
*Francis Bedford,
no.1811.* **CDV**
(G. Quinn collection)

A study titled the *Old Elm-Tree* (**53**) by Bedford shows the two familiar figures (probably his sons) and the tree otherwise known as the Cross Tree, as it grew out of a medieval cross base. The head of the cross is also visible. The tree was also known as the Dancing Tree as from about 1800 it became the support of dancing and music on a platform which could hold thirty people, an orchestra and six couples dancing! The old tree was blown over in 1903.[62]

54. The Old
Poor-House,
Moretonhampstead,
c.1865.
SX 755860.
*Francis Bedford,
no.1812.* **CDV**
(G. Quinn collection)

55. The Shambles,
Moretonhampstead,
c.1880.
SX 754861.
*Stereoscopic Gems,
English Scenery.* **SV**

A fine carte-de-visite photograph (**54**) by Bedford is labelled *The Old Poor-House* and shows a magnificent building then still in use as 'parish' accommodation. The date 1637 can be seen – this was when it underwent major renovation. High quality granite masonry and the fine arched arcade have given it a Grade I listing. The photograph shows the building before restoration 1938-1940.[63] Only six (out of ten) arches are visible. The second door in which the old woman (who is wearing a very old-fashioned bonnet) is standing, no longer exists.

'Stereoscopic Gems' published this view (**55**) of what was known as The Shambles in Moretonhampstead, perhaps in about 1880. Their printed label on the back commented that the town 'is remarkable for its salubrity, which may be inferred from the healthful looks of the inhabitants'. This is where butchers sold meat and farmers their dairy products. The building was sited in the middle of a busy junction, with Ford Street leading to Chagford on the right. It was demolished in about 1890.[64] Above the entrance can just be read the stencilled sign STICK NO BILLS.

56.
Raven's Tower/Tor,
Lustleigh Cleave,
looking west,
c. 1865.
SX 762819.
Francis Bedford,
Devonshire
Illustrated no. 1789.
SV
(stamp on reverse:
T. Way, Fine Art
Depot, Victoria
House, Torquay)

LUSTLEIGH CLEAVE

Black's *Guide* of 1864 (p.251) recommended visiting 'the lonesome valley of *Lustleigh Cleave*...and the ivy-shrouded rock called the Raven's Tower'. Francis Bedford's view (56) of this is of great interest as it is clearly influenced by a large painting (57) of Lustleigh Cleave by Francis

57.
Lustleigh Cleave,
c.1820 - painting
by *Francis Stevens,*
in Devon & Exeter
Institution, Exeter.
SX 762819
(approx)
(Photo: Philip
Kingslan John)

Stevens (1781-1822/3), who gave it to the Devon & Exeter Institution in 1820, where it still hangs.[65] The hatted figure sitting on the rock is in an almost identical pose in both images, the sheep are similarly positioned, and the lighting effects are also similar, so that it is reasonable to suppose that Bedford saw the painting in Exeter and was inspired to reproduce a version of it photographically in the mid-1860s. It is a classic example of photography imitating art. Also of interest in Bedford's view is that the bottom of the valley is completely bare of trees, while now it is thickly wooded.

At the higher end of Lustleigh Cleave lies Foxworthy, which was another Victorian tourist destination on account of its picturesque buildings. Bedford's wonderful carte-de-visite photograph (**58**) of the lane

58.
Lane to Foxworthy,
Manaton, c.1865.
SX 757821.
*Francis Bedford,
no. 1795.* **CDV**

59

59. Foxworthy
Bridge, Manaton,
c.1865.
SX 757821.
Francis Bedford,
Devonshire
Illustrated
no.1796. SV

leading to it is a masterpiece of composition and lighting, with the back-lit seated figure against a rustic fence, a rustic gate in the middle distance and the gable end of a thatched cottage behind. This was Little Silver, now completely gone. The lane is carried over a clapper bridge which is seen in this Bedford view (59) from below.

60. Rustic Bridge
with figures, Becky
Falls, Manaton,
c.1865.
 SX 760801.
Francis Bedford,
Devonshire
Illustrated
no.1799. **SV**

61. On the stream
above Becky Falls,
c.1865.
SX 760801.
Francis Bedford,
Devonshire
Illustrated
no.1800. **SV**

62. Manaton Green, c.1865. SX 750813. *William Spreat, 229 High Street, Exeter, no.566.* **SV**

MANATON

A short distance west of Lustleigh Cleave is Becka or Becky Falls. Bedford's views (60 and 61) of the timber clam bridge and of the stream above the falls are particularly impressive when viewed stereoscopically, as every leaf and rock appears three-dimensionally.

The village green at Manaton (62), photographed by Spreat, has changed remarkably little in 150 years. The young man on the right appears to be dressed in a postman's uniform of the early 1860s.

Bowerman's Nose is an iconic natural rock pillar, more than 30ft in height, near Manaton, north of Houndtor. The view (63) by William Spreat is from the south, and looks to neatly maintained enclosed fields on the slopes of Easdon beyond. Healthy heather is growing around the foot of the rock.

63. Bowermans Nose, Manaton, c.1865. SX 741805. *William Spreat, 229 High Street, Exeter, Stereoscopic Treasures no.374.* **SV**

64. Houndtor from
north-east, c.1865.
SX 743790 (tor).
Francis Bedford,
Devonshire
Illustrated no. 1803.
SV
(E. Greeves
collection)

HOUNDTOR AND HAYTOR AREA

Across the valley of the Becka Brook from Haytor, and very accessible, are
the remarkable rock formations of Houndtor, which were once also known
as Cluster Rocks.[66] An atmospheric view (**64**) by Bedford gives the tor a
somewhat Germanic or Scandinavian setting seen from the north-east
through trees, including conifers, reminiscent of the romantic paintings of
Caspar Friedrich. The figure is probably one of Bedford's sons. The roof of
a house can just be made out among the trees in the middle distance. The
view (**65**) of the tor from the
north, with the same figure, is of
interest because the vegetation
cover is significantly different
from that of today's broad closely-
grazed paths leading to the tor.
Spreat's carte-de-visite photograph (**66**), from the south, is
taken from near Hemsworthy
Gate and looks over the enclosure
walls of Emsworthy farm to
Holwell, with Houndtor and
Greator Rocks in the far distance.

65. Houndtor from
the north, c. 1865.
SX 743790.
Francis Bedford,
no. 1804. **CDV**

Haytor Rocks have long been a place of popular recreation, being the most massive and striking granite outcrops to be found on Dartmoor, within easy reach of the road. Francis Bedford captures the impressive bulk of the eastern rocks superbly in his photograph (67) by the careful positioning of figures – a man silhouetted on the top of the tor, and a man

66. Houndtor and Greator Rocks from near Hemsworthy Gate, c.1865.
SX 748760.
William Spreat, 229 High Street, Exeter, no. 782. **CDV**

67. Haytor – Eastern Rocks from the west, c.1865.
SX 758771.
Francis Bedford, no.1783. **CDV** (detail below)

68. Haytor –
Western Rocks
(Low Man) from
WSW, c.1865.
SX 757770.
*William Spreat, 229
High Street, Exeter
no. 785.* **CDV**
(detail below)

69. Haytor –
Western Rocks
(Low Man) from
the north, c.1865.
SX 757770.
*Francis Bedford,
Devonshire
Illustrated no.1784.*
SV

70. Haytor Rocks
from the east,
c.1865.
SX 758771.
Francis Bedford,
Devonshire
Illustrated no. 1782.
SV

71. Saddle Tor
from the west,
c.1865.
SX 751764.
William Spreat, 229
High Street, Exeter
no.786. **SV**

and woman at its base. William Spreat's view (68), with a figure stretched out in the foreground, is of the western rocks from the WSW. Bedford's two stereoscopic views (69 and 70) are striking for their unusual and imaginative viewpoints. Spreat also has an image (71) of Saddle Tor from the west (mislabelled *Heytor* on the original).

The 'Nutcracker' logan stone was a natural wonder a short distance south of Rippon Tor, estimated to weigh about 14 tons, but so finely balanced that it could be rocked. It was toppled in the early 1970s. It is interesting to see how Bedford and Spreat tackled the

72.
The 'Nutcracker'
Logan Stone,
Rippon Tor, from
SE, c.1865.
SX 744753. *Francis Bedford, no.1806.*
CDV

same subject. Bedford (72) has placed a person some distance from the stone to give an exaggerated impression of its size. Above the head of this figure is the indistinct shape of a building – this is Newhouse inn, now reduced to the faintest archaeological traces. In Spreat's view (73) the inn

73.
The 'Nutcracker'
Logan Stone,
Rippon Tor, from
SE, c.1865.
SX 744753.
William Spreat, 229 High Street, Exeter no. 675. **SV**

is also just visible and, on the hillside beyond, can be seen the prehistoric field system known as Foale's Arrishes. Mr Foale occupied Newhouse after the Leamans who were there in the 1820s. The last publican is said to have been a Hannaford. The inn had burnt down and was reduced to ruins before 1876.[67] Spreat leaves the underside of the stone clear of the horizon, thus emphasizing its bulk and poise.

PARKE

Precisely dated photographs are a rarity but this view (**74**) of the wedding of Emma Laetitia Parlby (1841-1926) to William Robert Hole (1831-1903) was taken on 8 April 1875. She was aged thirty-four, the second daughter of the Revd John and Emily Parlby of Manadon, Plymouth. William Hole was aged forty-four. His father had acquired the Parke estate in 1825. The couple were married at Pennycross, Plymouth.[68] The scene is outside Parke, Bovey Tracey, now the headquarters of Dartmoor National Park Authority. The wearing of a shawl by the lady third from left probably reflects the fact that it was early April. A particularly fine striped dress is visible on the right.

74. Parke, Bovey Tracey – the wedding of Emma Laetitia Parlby to William Robert Hole, 8 April 1875. SX 805786. *Anonymous*. **P**

75. Widecombe-in-the-Moor, from the west, early 1860s. SX 718768.
William Spreat, 229 High Street, Exeter no. 476. **SV**

WIDECOMBE-IN-THE-MOOR

Further into the moor is the remarkable settlement and valley of Widecombe-in-the-Moor. Spreat's view (**75**) from the west shows the setting of the village in the early 1860s, with the patchwork of fields on Widecombe Hill behind. Most of the visible buildings are thatched and the view shows the back of the Old Inn. The building on the left is on the site of the ancient manor house of North Hall. Bedford came here too and his finely composed image (**76**) shows the northern approach to the village from Natsworthy. In the heart of the village is the magnificent church house (**77**), used variously as an almshouse, school and community space. The roof is no longer thatched, the third upstairs window from the right has been altered to a gabled larger window, and the little lefthand window has been blocked up, but

76. Widecombe-in-the-Moor from the Natsworthy road, c.1865. SX 718768.
Francis Bedford, Devonshire Illustrated no. 2029. **SV**

77. Church House, Widecombe-in-the-Moor, c.1865. SX 719768. *Francis Bedford, Devonshire Illustrated no. 2030.* SV

otherwise it is instantly recognisable, as a superb building, probably of sixteenth-century date. Spreat's fine view (**78**) from inside the churchyard shows the lychgate (in which a girl is sitting) and the church house beyond in about 1865. I published a similar image in 1983, assigning it then, incorrectly, to the 1880s.[69]

78. Widecombe in the Moor - lych gate and Church House, c.1865. SX 719768. *William Spreat, 4 Gandy Street, Exeter.* SV
(detail below)

79. Buckland-in-the-Moor – the church from the south, c.1865.
SX 720731.
Francis Bedford, Devonshire Illustrated no. 2021.
SV

80. Buckland-in-the-Moor – cottage by the church, c.1865.
SX 720731.
Francis Bedford no.2022. **CDV**

81. Buckland-in-the-Moor – bridge and cottages, c.1865.
SX 725731.
Francis Bedford, Devonshire Illustrated no.2023.
SV

82. Buckland Bridge on the Webburn, c.1865.
SX 719719.
Francis Bedford, Devonshire Illustrated no.2018.
SV

BUCKLAND-IN-THE-MOOR

The tiny community of Buckland-in-the-Moor has also long been on the tourist trail. Bedford's skilful view (**79**) of the church seen from the south through a gate, and with a seated figure catching the light, is exquisite. The cottage by the church is another finely detailed picture (**80**). Quite different to later views which tend to focus on the quaint cottages about 400m east of the church, is Bedford's imaginative record (**81**) showing the bridge over the Ruddycleave Water, with the thatched roofs of the cottages behind. Buckland Bridge, over the River Webburn, just above its confluence with the River Dart, is seen in another lovely photograph (**82**), enhanced by the figures.

83. Eagle Rock,
Holne Chase, and
River Dart, c.1865.
SX 724724.
Francis Bedford,
Devonshire
Illustrated no.2010.
SV

HOLNE CHASE TO BUCKFAST

Opposite is the magnificent Holne Chase. The generally spectacular nature of the river scenery here is revealed in this photograph (83) by Bedford of Eagle Rock on the Holne side, looking downstream.

Another view (84) downstream shows the diagonal sweep of woodland on the Holne side and the crag of rock known as Lovers' Leap on the Buckland side. A. L. Coke of Newton Abbot published an image (85) of the same rock, but looking upstream. New Bridge (86) over the Dart, probably at least sixteenth-century in date[70] and so anything but new, marks the upper end of Holne Chase, which can be seen behind it.

84. Holne Chase
and Lovers' Leap,
c.1865.
SX 726723.
Francis Bedford.
Devonshire
Illustrated no.2012.
SV

85. Lovers' Leap,
The River Dart,
c.1865. SX
726723.
Archibald L. Coke.
Newton Abbot,
no. 245. **SV**

86. New Bridge,
River Dart, c.1865.
SX 712708.
Francis Bedford,
no.2024. **CDV**

87. Dart Bridge,
Buckfast, c.1860.
SX 745667.
Anonymous, but
probably *Way &*
Sons, Torquay. **SV**

Downstream by Buckfast is Dart Bridge seen in this early photograph (87), looking upstream, probably by Way & Sons. The clothing of the figure on the right suggests a date of about 1860 and perhaps even of the late 1850s. The photograph shows part of the medieval bridge which was widened in 1796 and 1827.[71]

Two-thirds of a mile downstream is Austin's Bridge, with a stone recording its builder (S. Meeffield) and the date 1749,[72] but now hardly noticed by traffic on the Totnes-Buckfastleigh road. A two-wheeled cart is visible on the bridge, with figures, in this photograph (88) by Bedford.

88. Austin's Bridge, River Dart, near Buckfastleigh, c.1865.
SX 750660.
Francis Bedford, Devonshire Illustrated no. 1994.
SV

89. Ivybridge,
River Erme,
c.1865.
SX 636564. *P. Yeo,
89 Union Street,
Plymouth.* SV

90. St John's
church, Ivybridge,
c.1865.
SX 635564.
George Fox. SV
(E. Greeves
collection)

IVYBRIDGE AND HARFORD

One of the most famous of Devon bridges, much visited by tourists and artists (including J. M. W. Turner) from the mid-eighteenth century onwards, was the single-arched Ivy Bridge which once carried the main road between Exeter and Plymouth across the River Erme.[73] Now a quiet backwater of Ivybridge, it was formerly renowned for its picturesque and sylvan beauty, captured here (89) by P. Yeo of Plymouth. Black's *Guide* of 1864 refers to it as 'ivy-shrouded' and as having a 'rude one-arched structure; wooded banks and lichen-covered rocks'.[74]

On the west side of the bridge was the church of St John, Ivybridge, built in 1789-1790 as a chapel-of-ease within Cornwood parish, photographed (90) by George Fox. A new church was built in 1881-1882, and the old church demolished in 1925, but its tower was retained.[75]

The impressive Stowford Paper Mills (91), recorded by W. Harding Warner of Bristol, produced high-quality paper from the end of the eighteenth century until closure in 2013. In 1849 the mill employed 60 men and 100 women which in the later nineteenth century had increased to a workforce of some 500 persons. The mill was reconstructed and enlarged between 1862 and 1867.[76] It is this new mill that is shown in the photograph, in its heyday, dominated by the tall rag loft of 1862.

The railway viaduct for Brunel's single track broad gauge South Devon railway, which reached Ivybridge in 1848, was much admired. This anonymous stereoview (92) is looking eastwards to Western Beacon, with Stowford House on the right of the image. The very end of the station platform can be seen on the extreme left. The viaduct clearly impressed the writer of Murray's *Handbook for Travellers to Devon & Cornwall* (1872),

91. Stowford Paper Mills, Ivybridge, c. 1865.
SX 636567.
W. Harding Warner, Bristol. **CDV**
(S. Bhanji collection)

92. Ivybridge Viaduct, c.1865. SX 635569. *Anonymous.* **SV**

who described it (p.106) as 'a spider-like fabric of such slender proportions that one wonders it has not long since been blown away into the moor. It resembles at a distance a line of tall chimneys, and consists of a black wooden roadway, which is carried in a curve over ten pairs of white granite pillars, each pair being 60 ft. apart, and the most elevated 115 ft. above the valley'. William Spreat's view (**93**) of the viaduct from below shows what a masterpiece of engineering and design it was. It was replaced in 1892 by a new viaduct beside it, carrying a double track standard gauge line.[77]

93. Ivybridge Viaduct from below, early 1860s. SX 635569. *William Spreat, 229 High Street, Exeter, Stereoscopic Treasures no. 124.* **SV**

94. Harford Bridge, River Erme, c.1865. SX 636596. *Anonymous.* **SV**

Two miles upstream of Ivybridge lies the small community of Harford which has had a stone bridge spanning the River Erme probably since medieval times.[78] This unattributed view (94) looks upstream towards the moor.

SHAUGH PRIOR AND DEWERSTONE
Shaugh Prior lies some seven miles north-west of Harford, as the crow flies. The ancient church of St Edward is seen in this photograph (95) from the north-west. Just under a mile downslope to the west

95. St Edward's Church, Shaugh Prior, c.1860. SX 543631. *Anonymous.* **CDV**

is Shaugh Bridge immediately below the confluence of the rivers Plym and Meavy. The present bridge is a rebuilding of 1825 following a storm in 1823,[79] and was another popular rendezvous for artists and visitors,

96. River Plym -
figures on rocks
below Shaugh
Bridge, c.1865
(detail).
SX 533635.
Anonymous. **SV**

97. Shaugh Bridge,
early 1860s.
SX 533635.
W. Heath & Co.,
Plymouth. **SV**

being described as 'an elegant structure of hewn granite' in Black's *Guide* of 1864. A detail from an early image (96) shows a standing man and three women sitting on rocks below the bridge. Although indistinct, their clothing is characteristic of the early 1860s. A winter view of the bridge (97) from upstream is by W. Heath & Co of Plymouth who were active photographers from the late 1850s, having advertised their 'Wholesale Photographic Depot' in Devonport in Billing's *Directory* of 1857.[80] On the left a track can be seen descending to the river and a presumed ford.

A short distance upstream from the confluence of the rivers is the Dewerstone, overlooking the Plym. This anonymous carte-de-visite (98) captures splendidly the setting of the 170ft (52m) high near-vertical face of Devil's Rock. It is taken from West Down looking across the River Plym approximately west-north-west to the valley of the River Meavy entering from the right, and to the slopes of Knowle Wood in the distance.

98. The Dewerstone, from West Down, c.1865. SX 539638. *Anonymous.* **CDV**

99.
The Dewerstone,
with leat launder,
c.1880.
SX 536638.
Frith Series. **P**

A view by Frith (**99**) is of special interest as it shows a wooden launder carrying water in the direction of a 16ft waterwheel working as part of an iron mine and brick manufactory, which was sited on the peninsula formed by the confluence of the two rivers. The date may be about 1880, when the 'Ferro-Ceramic Company Ltd', otherwise known as Dewerstone Iron Mine, was operating here. The launder is marked as 'Aqueduct' on the 1st edition Ordnance Survey 25-inch map published in 1886, by which time the mine was disused.[81]

YENNADON, SHEEPSTOR AND BURRATOR

In August 1873 a huge military exercise (the largest until the training of the Second World War) took place on Dartmoor. Some 12,000 troops participated in an event that was curiously known as the Autumn Manoeuvres (as it happened, they endured distinctly autumnal wet weather). Several photographs taken at the time have been published.[82] Much of the activity was on south-western Dartmoor. A view (**100**) shows an encampment on Yennadon Down as seen from Lynch Common, looking across Flat Wood and the valley of the River Meavy. A specially

100. Military Camp on Yennadon Down, from Lynch Common ('Camp of 1st Division Yannaton'), August 1873. SX 545678. *Anonymous*. **P**

101. Military
Butchery,
Yennadon Down
('Commissariat
Establishment'),
with view to Lynch
Common, August
1873. SX 543677.
Anonymous. **P**
(detail below)

fine photograph (**101**) shows the 'Commissariat Establishment' on
Yennadon Down looking southwards to the cottage by Marchants Cross,
Wigford Down and, in the distance, Saddlesborough. A massive timber
framework holds the carcasses of slaughtered cattle. Another beast is
about to be pole-axed. These are not Devon cattle and presumably

accompanied the troops on their journey to Dartmoor. The man leaning nonchalantly against the poles of a cart on the extreme left is smoking a pipe. Beside him are scales of some sort suspended from a tripod and chains. An engraving (102) reproduced on the front page of *The Graphic* on 16 August 1873, titled 'The Butcher's Shop', shows cattle carcasses hanging from a frame and an identical cart to that in the photograph, and seems clearly based on this scene.

102. 'The Butcher's Shop', *The Graphic*, 16 August 1873, engraving

One mile to the east of this spot is the little village of Sheepstor seen in this stereoview (103) probably taken by William Merrifield of Tavistock, looking north-east from a gateway onto Portland Lane. The scene of the church tower, and the backdrop of Sheepstor itself (originally

103. St Leonard's Church, Sheepstor, early 1860s. SX 560677. *William Merrifield* [?]. **SV**

Scitelstor, and variant spellings, possibly meaning 'steep tor'), has
changed relatively little today. In about 1846, probably no more than
twenty years before this photograph was taken, Rachel Evans visited
Sheepstor. She was distinctly underwhelmed, recording that there was
'little to interest in the place'. Worse still she and her companions
ventured into an inn ('the rudest I have ever entered') where the 'little
farmers...had never heard of events which were common in the mouths of
all civilized communities'. Their apparent ignorance appalled her and she
launched into a diatribe on the slovenliness and filth of their dwellings
and lives, urging that 'an enlightened morality be enforced'.[83]

An ancient lane led from Sheepstor to Walkhampton and beyond,
crossing the River Meavy on a single-arched bridge, seen in an
unattributed view (**104**). The bridge now lies below the waters of Burrator
Reservoir (completed 1898). About a mile upstream is Nosworthy Bridge
(**105**), still in use. However, the open landscape towards Leather Tor,
dimly seen on the horizon, can no longer be appreciated due to trees and
coniferous plantations. Part of the simpler bridge over the Newleycombe
Lake is seen on the right. Less than half a mile further upstream, still on

105. Nosworthy Bridge, River Meavy, early 1860s. SX 568695. *Anonymous*. **SV**

106. Leather Tor Bridge, River Meavy, early 1860s. SX 569699. *Anonymous*. **SV**

the River Meavy, is the remarkable Leather Tor Bridge (106), built by George Worth and William Mashford in the style of a traditional clapper bridge as late as 1855, to replace use of the ford and stepping stones known as 'Redipit Steps'.[84] The substantial cut and dressed blocks of granite used for the bridge and its massive parapets are unusual. The frequency of bridges here reflects the busy traffic along routes which connected numerous ancient farms in the vicinity, all of which had been abandoned by the late nineteenth century or first three decades of the twentieth century.

107. Grimstone,
Horrabridge –
summerhouse and
garden, c.1865.
SX 515706.
*R. P. Yeo, 8
Devonshire Terrace,
Plymouth.* **SV**

HORRABRIDGE AND GRENOFEN

At Horrabridge, between Yelverton and Tavistock, is Grimstone Manor
where a fine rustic summerhouse and formal garden (**107**) existed when the
large house and grounds were owned by Sir Robert Porrett Collier Esq.,
MP (1817-1886). He was the eldest son of John Collier (1769-1849) who
had bought Grimstone Manor in 1814. Robert Collier was a significant
legal figure in the mid-nineteenth century being Solicitor General for
England & Wales 1863-66 and Attorney General 1868-71. He was
Member of Parliament for Plymouth 1852-1871.[85] He was much involved
with local mining and wrote an important *Treatise on the Law Relating to
Mines* (1849). The summerhouse still survives but is much neglected.

The 'long and lofty timber viaduct' at Grenofen [86] was designed by
Brunel and carried the South Devon & Tavistock Railway over the
Walkham valley. It was 1,100 feet long with seventeen spans and was

completed in 1859. It is seen here in a fine image (**108**) by Merrifield, looking towards Grenofen, probably soon after its completion.

108. Grenofen Viaduct, River Walkham, c.1860. SX 495705. *William Merrifield, Tavistock.* **SV** (Merrifield Collection, Tavistock Museum)

TAVISTOCK

Tavistock in the nineteenth century was an extraordinarily busy place, thanks largely to the mining industry of west Devon and the Tamar valley. The population of the town and surrounding parish reached a peak of nearly 9,000 in 1861, having risen progressively from about 3,500 at the beginning of the century, and declining thereafter until modern times.[87] The Dukes of Bedford, whose family had acquired the Abbey lands in the sixteenth century, were responsible for major redevelopment in the centre of the town in the 1850s and 1860s. Some of this was recorded by pioneer photographer William Merrifield who was librarian of the Tavistock Subscription Library.

109. Bedford
Hotel, Tavistock,
from churchyard,
c.1860.
SX 482744.
*William Merrifield,
Tavistock.* **SV**

The front of the Bedford Hotel (**109**) on Plymouth Road was recorded
by Merrifield in about 1860, from the parish churchyard. The hotel had
evolved from an early eighteenth-century private house, with alterations
by Wyatville and Foulston 1822-30.[88] It features in Anthony Trollope's
novel *The Three Clerks* (1858): 'I beg to assure any travelling readers that
they might have drunk tea in a much worse place' (1907 edn, p.82). Some
of the characters described in the novel would fit well these six men up
against the railings in Bedford Square in this image (**110**) by Furze. The
range of hats is remarkable – top hats were made at Mr Doidge's premises
at the top of Love Lane (now North Street) and Mr Colwell owned another
'hatter's works' in Kilworthy Lane.[89] The tower of the parish church is

(opposite)
110. Tavistock – six men and parish church, c.1865. SX 482744. *Furze.* **SV**
(detail below)

without its four crockets, but in this anonymous stereoview (111) two of them are clearly seen.

All four crockets are visible in this interesting stereoview (112) looking up West Street from Bedford Square, which has an ownership inscription dated 1866. The photograph was published by W. Robjohns of Tavistock. A sign for The Commercial Inn projects over the pavement.

This superb photograph (113) looking down West Street in about 1865 is anonymous, but admirably captures the feel of the period, and the remarkable array of shop fronts.

111. Tavistock
Parish Church,
c. 1865.
SX 482744.
Anonymous. **SV**

112. Parish church
and West Street,
Tavistock, from
Bedford Square,
c. 1865.
SX 482745.
*W. Robjohns,
Tavistock.* **SV**

113. Looking down West Street, Tavistock, c. 1865. SX 477742. *Anonymous*. **CDV** (G. Quinn collection)

The crockets on the church tower look very new. Just distinguishable when viewing the original with a magnifying glass is a sign behind the lamp-post halfway down the righthand side, reading SPURREL'S Coffee HOUSE. In 1857[90] Samuel Spurrell was listed as a 'shoemaker and coffee-house keeper' in Higher Brook Street but by 1866[91] had 'coffee rooms' as well as still being a shoemaker, in West Street. By the end of the 1870s he was 'shoemaker and refreshment house keeper' at 16 West Street.[92]

The imposing and distinctive Fitzford Church (114), on the western edge of the town on the road towards Gunnislake, has been a

114. Fitzford Church, Tavistock, c.1865. SX 474739. *Furze*. **SV**

Roman Catholic church since 1952, but was built 1865-1867 as an Anglican church, to cater for the then expanding mining population. Its architect was Henry Clutton who combined 'Lombardic Romanesque with Transitional Gothic'.[93] The view by Furze was probably taken soon after completion. T. Vanstone in 1914 remembered that in the 1840s, on the south-east side of the site of what was to be the 'New Church' [i.e. Fitzford], there was a tithe barn and

> On the mound just beyond the barn the remains of mine workings were then in evidence, among them a portion of a horse-whim, used for raising whatever was needed from the adjoining shaft. The old Fitzford Archway [i.e. gatehouse] was then in a sad state of repair. The roof was entirely gone, having fallen in, and the back and side walls gave notice of an early collapse. The archway was partly blocked with rubbish, and a large portion of the ground in front was used as a stone breaking depot... At the back of the building was an old farm-house and a good size orchard, together with outhouses, some of which were attached to the archway. Photographs of the building taken at this date are still extant. Afterwards the old structure was taken down, the stones numbered, and the building re-erected as it now stands, the cost being defrayed by the then Duke of Bedford'.[94]

The mine workings were those of Wheal Pixon.[95]

The Fitzford Gatehouse was once the imposing entrance to Fitzford, a mansion built by the Fitz family. All traces of the mansion had gone by the early 1860s but in 1869 the gatehouse was demolished before being rebuilt on the same site by 1871.[96] A view (**115**) by Merrifield probably

115. Fitzford Gatehouse, Tavistock, c.1865. SX 475739. *William Merrifield, Tavistock.* **CDV**

dates to around 1865 as it shows stoneworkers as mentioned by Vanstone (above). In the background are Fitzford Cottages, part of a group of thirty-six dwellings newly built in 1862.[97]

Lady Howard's Oak is shown in an image (**116**) by Furze. It bordered the River Tavy and may well be the one referred to by Rachel Evans in 1846 as 'a withered oak, spreading out young and vigorous branches, even though the very heart of its trunk is decayed'.[98] Lady Mary Howard (1596-1671) was the daughter of suicide John Fitz of Fitzford and had a troubled life, marrying four times. Her last husband was Sir Richard Grenville, who treated her cruelly. Her spirit is said to travel to Okehampton Castle to bring back a blade of grass, one at a time, to Tavistock, but what her connection is with this tree is unknown.[99]

116. Tavistock – Lady Howard's Oak, River Tavy, Tavistock, c. 1865. SX 479740 (approx.) *Furze.* SV

117. Tavistock
Canal, with figure
by gate, c.1865.
SX 473726
(approx.).
Furze. **SV**
(detail below)

A view (117) by Furze on the Tavistock Canal is possibly the earliest
photographic image (about 1865) we have of this remarkable feat of
engineering, designed by John Taylor and built 1803-1817, to link
Tavistock and west Dartmoor mines with the port at Morwellham,
accessible by ocean-going ships. A fine patriarchal figure is shown by a
rustic gate, with the water of the canal on the left. The scene may be close
to Crowndale Farm.

On the south-western edge of Victorian Tavistock, between the
Whitchurch Road and the Plymouth Road was Wheal Crelake, a large
and important copper mine, which also produced some argentiferous lead,
and some arsenic. This highly important photograph (118) was probably
taken by William Merrifield. A letter from James Mildren to Miss Rosa
M. Merrifield dated 7 December 1973 mentions 'a hitherto unknown
picture of Tavistock's Crelake Mine' among 90 photographic glass slides
by William Merrifield, which had been sent from South Africa by a cousin
of Miss Merrifield.[100] Two chimneys of Fitzford Cottages built in 1862 are
visible bottom left, and the view looks south-eastwards. The mine began

Wheal Crelake. Tavistock.

work in the late 1850s. In April 1860 the mine was said to be conducted in 'a splendid...luxurious, style'. The chimney stack, said in 1861 to be reminiscent of Nelson's Column, was part of an engine house for a variety of steam-driven machinery. Davey's Shaft, the headgear of which is visible in the centre of the image, was by 1862 some 86 fathoms (516 ft) deep, and eventually reached 116 fathoms (696 ft). No fewer than 270 persons were employed at its peak. It closed in the mid-1870s.[101] In the lower centre of the picture is the toll-house at the junction of Plymouth Road and Pixon Lane, built in about 1822 and still extant.[102]

118. Crelake Mine, Tavistock, early 1860s. SX 479736.*William Merrifield* [?] **P.** (copy in G. Perkins collection)

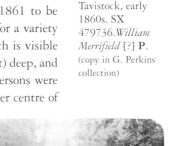

Before the new turnpike road was constructed in 1817 [103], following the valley of the River Tavy upstream, the road from the centre of Tavistock towards Exeter took a higher route, now known as Old Exeter Road. Just below Wilminstone Quarry there was a crossroads known as Twobridges. Two views (**119** and **120**) look north-east and

119. Twobridges, Wilminstone, Tavistock, looking north-east on Old Exeter Road, c.1865. SX 492755. *Furze.* **SV**

120. Twobridges, Wilminstone, Tavistock, looking south-west on Old Exeter Road, c.1865. SX 492755. *William Merrifield* [?]. SV (Merrifield Collection, Tavistock Museum)

south-westwards towards Tavistock respectively. Some of the buildings seen are still extant, though modified. The 'Old House' in Furze's view is now known as Orchard Cottage.

MERRIVALE, ROOS TOR AND PEW TOR

The road from Tavistock to Princetown crosses the River Walkham at Merrivale Bridge. A photograph (121) by Frith, dating from about 1871, looks towards Merrivale Bridge from the east. In the foreground is a fine prehistoric hut circle, one of a large group still extant here. On the further hillslope can be seen Merrivale Farm which is of medieval origin. On the right of the photograph are three buildings. The topmost became a Post

121. Prehistoric hut circle, Merrivale, c.1871. SX 555750. *Francis Frith's Carte Series no.*5790. **CDV**

Office. Below it is the Dartmoor Inn, and below that is a roofless barn known as Lang's Barn – this had been reroofed by the early years of the twentieth century. The photograph predates the start of Merrivale Quarry in 1875 as no infrastructure, such as a road for the quarry, is visible, nor is there any quarry spoil.

High above the Walkham, on its west side, is Roos Tor, seen here in a stereoview (**122**) by Merrifield (sent to the author by an artist friend in

122. Roos Tor, early 1860s. SX 543767. *William Merrifield, Tavistock.* **SV**

Newfoundland!). It is remarkable that the photographer took his
equipment 2km (1¼ miles) into the moor to record this shot, but he
would have been familiar with the location, having taught in a school at
relatively nearby Peter Tavy between 1832-1838, when he lived in Peter
Tavy Combe.[104] Another striking tor near Tavistock is Pew Tor,
photographed here (**123**) by Furze.

LYDFORD

Eight miles north of Tavistock is Lydford, the ancient medieval capital of
Dartmoor with its twelfth century 'castle' and stannary prison, but also
famed for the remarkable gorge through which the River Lyd flows. At
the south end of the gorge the river is joined by a stream cascading over
the White Lady Falls. This was another favourite attraction for artists and
other visitors from the late eighteenth century onwards. As Smiles &
Pidgley[105] point out, although a relatively modest waterfall, it featured as
the frontispiece illustration to the sumptuous *Devonshire & Cornwall
Illustrated* (1832) by Britton and Brayley, who wrote that 'all the
accompaniments' of the secluded spot 'are calculated to inspire feelings of
deep and chastened pleasure'.[106] Henry Hayman, a pioneer photographer
of Launceston, captured a fine view (**124**) of the falls (which could be

124. White Lady Falls, Lydford Gorge, c.1875. SX 501834. *Henry Hayman, Launceston.* **CDV**

125. Bridge in Lydford Gorge, c.1865. SX 505842 (approx.). *Furze.* **SV** (detail below)

enhanced if a miller released water over it). In the gorge itself Furze recorded this fine rustic bridge and gentleman (**125**).

MELDON

Spanning the steep-sided West Okement River on the north-west side of Dartmoor, is the elegant, almost delicate, Meldon Viaduct, known as 'The Spider Bridge' to local people when it was built. A contemporary account described it as 'a graceful as well as a remarkable structure. The railway is poised in mid-air...' .[107] This view (**126**), looking downstream, is by Henry Hayman, probably about the time it was opened, in October 1874. The viaduct was built by contractor Robert Thomas Relf for the Devon & Cornwall Railway Co., with ironwork supplied by Rownson, Drew & Co. of London. It is 560 ft long and reaches 154 ft above the river. It has six spans each of 90 ft on five piers

of wrought iron girders with two cast-iron 'column abutments'.[108] As seen in this photograph, it was a single track. A second track, on a cast iron framework, was completed in September 1879.[109] On the west side of the river, above the retaining wall, can be seen two buildings of a lime quarry before a large kiln was constructed behind the lefthandmost building. [110]

126. Meldon Viaduct, West Okement, c.1875. SX 565924. *Henry Hayman, Launceston.* **SV**

127. 'Lady Chapel', Okehampton Castle, c.1875. SX 584943. *Francis Frith's Carte Series no.3583.* **CDV**

OKEHAMPTON

Two miles downstream from the viaduct is Okehampton Castle, the romantically ruined seat of the Courtenay family, long admired for its 'picturesque' qualities.[111] A view by Frith of the Chapel (**127**) of about AD 1300 illustrates well the Victorian taste for crumbling ivy-clad ruins, which would be much frowned upon by today's English Heritage.

SOUTH ZEAL

To complete the circuit of the moor, returning to its north-east flank, is the remarkable village of South Zeal which still retains much of the physical structure of its medieval status as a borough founded at the end of the thirteenth century. This photograph (**128**) has been published before[112] when I suggested a date of '1880s or earlier', but its style and appearance now make me suggest a date of the 1860s. It is by an unknown photographer, and shows cottages, between the old market cross and the medieval chapel of St Mary, which were apparently demolished in 1877.[113] The cottages are also shown in a watercolour by Samuel Prout dated to 1806.[114]

128. South Zeal, c.1870. SX 651936. *Anonymous.* **P**

A Mystery Photograph

The recognition of some images can be full of challenges. The location of this early photograph (**129**), which appears to be an archetypal scene of Dartmoor moorland landscape, has not yet been identified. A light two-wheeled horse-drawn vehicle has brought a group of people to a moorland stream beside a substantial single-storey building which one might imagine had an industrial purpose. Two women are dressed in clothes of the late 1850s or early 1860s. Three other figures are visible. The original image was produced as a stereoview, and is now in the Howarth-Loomes collection, originally catalogued only as 'Dartmoor, view'.[115] Bernard and Alma Howarth-Loomes were both important collectors of early photography, especially stereoscopic images.

129. Moorland location by stream, with building and figures, c.1860. **SV** (Howarth-Loomes Collection, National Monuments Record/BB70/1577)

TO TOURISTS AND VISITORS

TO THE

WEST OF ENGLAND.

FIRST-CLASS

PHOTOGRAPHS AND STEREOGRAPHS

OF THE

PRINCIPAL OBJECTS OF INTEREST IN THE COUNTIES
OF DEVON AND CORNWALL,

PUBLISHED BY

W. SPREAT,

229, HIGH ST., EXETER.

Amongst the places thus illustrated are Lynton and Lynmouth, Ilfracombe,
Bideford, and Clovelly, in North Devon; Exeter and its Cathedral, Dawlish,
Teignmouth, Torquay, Ivy Bridge, Plymouth, Devonport, and Mount Edgecumbe,
South Devon; Penzance, St. Michael's Mount, the Logan Rock and Land's End
District, Kynance Cove and the Lizard District, Truro, Falmouth, Liskeard, and St.
Germain's, in Cornwall.

Constant additions of new subjects will be made to the list, which at present
contains more than 300.

A GREAT VARIETY OF

**LITHOGRAPHIC PRINTS OF NORTH AND SOUTH DEVON, AND
THE CATHEDRAL, EXETER.**

TO SOLICITORS, SURVEYORS,

AND

ESTATE AGENTS.

Drawings and Plans of Estates

EXECUTED IN THE BEST STYLE OF LITHOGRAPHY,

BY

W. SPREAT,

ARTIST AND LITHOGRAPHER,

229, HIGH STREET, AND 2, GANDY STREET,

EXETER.

EVERY KIND OF LITHOGRAPHY, ARTISTIC AND COMMERCIAL;
Book Illustrations, Drawings of all kinds, Plans, Show Cards, Labels, Cheques, Drafts,
Mining Forms, Bill Heads, Circulars, Cards, &c., &c.
ESTIMATES SENT ON APPLICATION.

THE PHOTOGRAPHERS

Photography in Devonshire could arguably be said to have begun with William Henry Fox Talbot's image taken from Mount Edgcumbe looking towards Devonport in 1845[116] and the photographic print (he called it a 'Sun-Picture' or 'Talbotype'), also from Mount Edgcumbe, published in June 1846 in *The Art-Union*.[117]

That photography was becoming well-established in Devon by the mid-1850s is indicated by the range of commercial establishments listed in Billing's *Directory* published in 1857.[118] Several photographic establishments in Plymouth & Devonport placed advertisements in the *Directory* – including portraiture studios of The London Photographic Company (Barclay & Co), which also had premises in Exeter (p.153); Messrs Smith & Co who described themselves as 'Photographic Artists' and who had 'Photographic Rooms' in Union Street (p.156); William C. Cox whose 'Photographic Department' in Devonport sold cameras and chemicals (p.169); and W. Heath who had a 'Wholesale Photographic Depot' also in Devonport (p.172) – the latter advertised cameras 'for portraits or landscapes', besides chemicals, papers etc.

In Exeter Owen Angel had a 'photographic institution' (p.43). Beard's 'Photographic Institution' (p.45), Charles Hart 'artist and photographer' (p.52), A. De Nicéville 'photographic artist' (p.57), James Tremlett 'photographic artist' (p.63), and John Walker, 'photographic artist' in Gandy Street, Exeter (p.64), were all listed. The 'photographic gallery' of Barclay and Groom in the High Street, Exeter was a late addition to the *Directory*.[119]

Britton & Son had held a photographic exhibition in Barnstaple in 1855[120] and Beard's [erroneously printed Bearo's] had advertised as photographers as early as January 1855.[121] The Devon & Exeter Photographic Society was established by the mid-1850s.[122]

Already by 1866 no fewer than seventy-eight photographers were listed in Devon in Kelly's *Directory*[123] – these included Owen Angel of Exeter; J. Brinley of Totnes; A. L. Coke of Newton Abbot; W. Heath of Plymouth; and W. Widger of Torquay; besides J. Coombe of Okehampton and H. Eddy of Ashburton.

In Kelly's *Directory* of 1883 seventy photographers were listed in the county, including Owen Angel in Exeter; Brinley & Son in Totnes; J. Chennall, jun. in Tavistock and W. Widger of Torquay.[124]

Sarah Fox's *Kingsbridge Estuary* (1864) was one of the first books on Devon to be published with photographic prints. Duprez included prints in *Duprez's trip up the Tamar* (1870) and Francis Bedford (see below) published several books of photographic prints of Devon from the late 1860s onwards such as *Photographic Views of Devonshire* (c. 1868).

(Bracketed numbers refer to pictures in this book.)

OWEN ANGEL (c.1821-1909) Exeter (49), was born in Totnes. He was established as a photographer in Exeter by the mid-1850s, having previously worked from the early 1840s as an engraver, printer and lithographer. He married Mary Ann Brimacombe in Exeter in 1843.[125] He received medals from the Birmingham Photographic Society in 1861 and from the Photographic Society of Great Britain in 1877.[126]

FRANCIS BEDFORD (1815-1894), London (6, 8, 15, 21, 22, 27, 32, 33, 38, 51, 52, 53, 54, 56, 58, 59, 60, 61, 64, 65, 67, 69, 70, 72, 76, 77, 79, 80, 81, 82, 83, 84, 86, 88). Undoubtedly the most important early landscape photographer in Devon was Francis Bedford. His significance lies not only in the large number of images which have survived, but in his remarkable artistic and technical skills of composition. His stereoviews published in the 'Devonshire Illustrated' series, and as cartes-de-visite published with the same serial numbers, are of the greatest importance, and were clearly designed for the commercial market. Many are reproduced in this book. He produced similar series of Herefordshire, Monmouthshire, Warwickshire and North Wales.

131.
Francis Bedford
(Wellcome Library,
London 24570.i)

Nationally renowned as a photographer in his lifetime, according to Sophie Gordon he 'probably made over 3,000 stereoscopic views between the late 1850s and c.1867, although most date to the period between 1857 and 1862'.[127] Like Angel and Spreat, his early career was as a lithographer. He wrote extensively on photographic technique, and was a proponent of the collodion wet-plate process (invented in 1851) for negatives, and albumen prints.

JOHN BRINLEY (c.1815 – c.1882), Fore Street, Totnes (2). John Brinley was aged forty-six at the time of the census of 1861 in which he is listed as a photographer, having been born in Exeter. His son Jeffery John was listed, aged seventeen, as a 'Photographer's Assistant' in the census of 1871. Both father and son were practising as photographers in 1881.

T. BRINLEY, Totnes (31) – no independent record of a T. Brinley has yet been found. The printed card (on right) may be an error for J. Brinley, though this seems unlikely.

ROBERT BURNARD (1848-1920), Plymouth and Hexworthy (1). Burnard's photographic work is a generation later than most of the images in this book, but is of the greatest importance as a fine social and documentary record of Dartmoor at the end of the nineteenth century.[128]

255   SOUTH DEVON.

The River Dart,—Dartmeet Bridge.

Photographed and Published by A. L. COKE, Newton-Abbot, Devon.

ARCHIBALD L. COKE (1824-1896), Courtenay Park, Newton Abbot (7, 47, 85). He also produced photographs under the name of Cocke. Some of his stereoviews were published by J. Chapple of Newton Abbot. He had a photographic studio in London in the mid-1850s, but was working in Cornwall, Isles of Scilly and Devon by the early 1860s.[129] However, his career did not always run smoothly as he was discharged from bankruptcy as a 'Photographic Artist' of East Wonford, Devon in April 1862.[130]

GEORGE FOX (c.1815- ?) (90). It is tempting to suggest that George Fox can be identified as the photographer brother of Sarah Prideaux Fox. Recorded as a retired dentist in the census returns of 1861 and 1871, living with his sister in Kingsbridge, he was the photographer of the images published in her pioneer book on that south Devon town.[131] He was born in Perranarworthal, Cornwall in about 1815, which was the industrial base for the famous Fox family of Quakers.[132]

FRANCIS FRITH (1822-1898), Surrey (35, 44, 45, 99, 121, 127). Frith was a leading national photographer of the nineteenth century, establishing a studio in Surrey from 1859.

FURZE, Tavistock (**110, 111, 114, 116, 117, 119, 123, 125**). Nothing has yet been discovered about this photographer.

HENRY HAYMAN, Church Street, Launceston (**124, 126**). Charles Thomas suggests that Hayman began professional photographic work in the late 1850s. Joined by his son in about 1870, the business continued until the early 1890s.[133]

WILLIAM HEATH (1823- ?), George Street, Plymouth (**97**). Described as 'one of the best-known Plymouth photographers',[134] he was working from at least the mid-1860s onwards,[135] sometimes as W. Heath & Co.

132. William Merrifield at Kilworthy Hill (V. Noonan collection)

WILLIAM MERRIFIELD (1804-1885), Tavistock (**11, 103, 108, 109, 115, 118, 120, 122**). Born in Tavistock to Samuel and Sarah Merrifield in 1804, he married Ann Sargent in 1832 in the same year that he took on a teaching role in Peter Tavy. From 1838 he and his family lived in Tavistock. By 1840 he was recorded as an engraver. The following year he became librarian of the Tavistock Subscription Library (then known as the Public Library) – a post he kept until 1872. In retirement he lived in Laurel Cottage on Kilworthy Hill.[136] As an early photographer of Tavistock and west Dartmoor he is an important figure recording, for example, the demolition of buildings for the Duke of Bedford's remodelling of the centre of Tavistock in the late 1850s.[137] In the *Tavistock Gazette* of 7 September 1866 he placed an advertisement (**134**) for his 'just published' series of 'New Photographs of Tavistock' sold by G. Spencer, bookseller and stationer at 8d each. His obituary in the *Tavistock Gazette*, 30 January 1885 refers to his 'love of science' but, curiously, makes no mention of his pioneer photographic work from the late 1850s and 1860s.

W. ROBJOHNS, Tavistock (112). Nothing is known of him as a photographer and it may be that he was primarily the publisher of other people's work from the mid-1860s. In 1870 William Robjohns was listed in West Street as a 'house decorator, bookseller, stationer, paper-hanger and agent to the Liverpool, London and Globe Insurance Company', in Morris & Co's *Commercial Directory & Gazetteer* of that year.

WILLIAM SPREAT (1816 - ?), Exeter (3, 4, 5, 9, 10, 13, 19, 24, 25, 26, 32, 37, 48, 50, 62, 63, 66, 68, 71, 73, 75, 78, 93). William Spreat was born in 1816, the son of an Exeter bookseller. In the 1840s he was a leading lithographer, especially of Devon church scenes.[138] In 1862 he published an advertisement (130) in Harrison, Harrod & Co's *Postal Directory & Gazetteer of Cornwall & Devon* addressed to 'Tourists and Visitors to the West of England' offering more than 300 'First-Class Photographs and Stereographs of the principal objects of interest in the counties of Devon and Cornwall'. This shows that his stereoscopic images were already very much a commercial venture by this date. His address in the advertisement was given as 229 High Street,Exeter, with this and other premises at 2 Gandy Street offering artistic and lithographic products, though in a separate listing in the same directory (p.63) his address is

133. William Spreat
(G. Falvey collection)

given as 27 Gandy Street. His Devon stereoviews have printed stamps on the reverse, which most commonly give 229 High Street, Exeter as his address and sometimes with 'Stereoscopic Treasures' in a circle. Charles Thomas states that these are his earlier images, and that he later had premises at 254 High Street and 4 Castle Street.[139] His Devon stereoviews also record 4 Gandy Street. Many, though not all, of the cards have a printed number on the front. Two of Haytor are numbered 785 and 786, which are the highest numbers noted so far. Presumably those numbered below 300 can be considered relatively early, i.e. 1862 or earlier in date. Thomas infers[140] that Spreat printed the work of several photographers, at least for Cornish scenes, but this has not yet been verified for Devon. Like Coke, he was discharged from bankruptcy in 1869.[141]

James Valentine (1814-1879), Dundee (36). A nationally important photographer, especially of Scotland, from the 1850s, based in premises in Dundee.

W. Harding Warner (1816-1894), Bristol (91). In the 1860s he was based in Ross, Herefordshire. He recorded several scenes in Devon, including Torquay and Plymouth.

Way & Sons, Victoria Parade, Torquay (16, 23, 30, 87). Working extensively in the 1860s, and very probably from the late 1850s too, this firm was based in premises overlooking the harbour. Their stereoviews of the Torbay area often had elaborate printed labels.[142]

P. Yeo, 89 Union Street, Plymouth (89). Scott does not list a P. Yeo as a photographer under Plymouth, though he gives a Richard Yeo at 89 Union Street in 1865.[143]

Richard P. Yeo (c.1825-?), 8 Devonshire Terrace, Plymouth (107). Scott[144] lists several members of the Yeo family as photographers in Plymouth from 1862-1910. R. P. Yeo was active as a portrait photographer from the late 1850s[145] and as a landscape photographer from the 1860s.[146]

134.
Advertisement by
William Merrifield
in 1866

JUST PUBLISHED BY MR. W. MERRIFIELD,
A SERIES OF

NEW PHOTOGRAPHS

OF

TAVISTOCK :

AMONG WHICH WILL BE FOUND

Bedford Square, shewing the New Hall; Abbey Bridge and Weir Head; the Abbey Archway from the South; the Abbey Archway, Guildhall, and Bedford Square; the New Hall; Tavistock Church from Bedford Square; Steps on the Tavy; the Still House and the Tavy; the Abbey Weir from the Walks; Tavistock Church and Tower from the Plymouth Road; &c., &c.

SOLD BY

G. SPENCER,

BOOKSELLER, STATIONER, &c.,

BEDFORD SQUARE, TAVISTOCK.

8d. each.

REFERENCES

1   Greeves & Somers Cocks, 1983
2   Burnard, 1890-94
3   Greeves, 2004
4   Greeves, 2004, p.72 lower
5   Greeves, 2004, p.87 upper
6   Thomas, 1988
7   Sumner, 2010
8   Gordon, 2013; Spencer, 2011
9   Rowe, 1848, 87
10 Croker, 1852, 16
11 Bedford, 1867, cited in Gordon, 2013
12 Matthew, 2010
13 Gray, 2001
14 Greeves & Stanbrook, 2004
15 Greeves, 1996, 86
16 pers. comm. Fred Willcocks, 25 May 2001
17 Thomas, 1992, 179
18 Risdon, 1811 edn, 223
19 Bhanji, 2010, 228
20 Crossing, 1901, 97
21 Proctor & Spooner, 1980, Plate IIa
22 Brodie et al, 2002, 139, 141; Joy, 2002, Vol.2, 133-141
23 Lewis, 1821
24 see Greeves 1986, plates 25 & 26
25 Greeves, 1986, 23
26 cf. Newman, 2002, 32
27 Broughton 1968/9, 27
28 Ravenhill, 1965, 8
29 Gray & Rowe, eds, 1997, 14-15
30 Gray & Rowe, 1997,15
31 Polwhele, 1793, 56
32 Polwhele,1793,57
33 Swete, 1796, 115 -7
34 Warner, 1800, 174-176
35 Rowe, 1830, 188
36 Rowe, 1848, 105
37 Halloran, J., 1996, 95-6
38 Black, 1864, 200
39 Gosse, 1865, 379
40 Black, 1864, 200
41 Mildren, 1984, 86-7
42 Black, 1864, 200; Murray, 1872, 133
43 Museum of English Rural Life, Reading/SEP/DEV 28)
44 MS notebook by W. H. Worth in possession of author
45 Stanbrook, 1990
46 Chapple, 1779; Polwhele, 1793, 65-95
47 Swete, 1796, 110-112, fig. opp. p.110
48 Lysons, 1822, cccviii
49 Ormerod, 1872
50 Ormerod, 1872, 347
51 Ormerod, 1871, 408
52 Gordon, 2013, 21, 32
53 Hayter-Hames, 1981, 80
54 Harris, 1968, 119-120
55 Crossing, 1902, 137
56 Hayter-Hames, 1981, plate 26
57 Ormerod, 1876, 72-3
58 Gray, 2001, 24-25
59 Greeves, 2014
60 Kelly, 1866, 912
61 Moretonhampstead History Society website
62 Friend, 1989, 25
63 Friend, 1989, 22-23; Hardiman and Mortimer, n.d. (c.2012), 51-53
64 Friend, 1989, 28

65 Smiles & Pidgley, 1995, 97-8

66 Croker, 1852, 10

67 Hemery, 1983, 660-661

68 *Western Times* 10 April 1875

69 Greeves & Somers Cocks, 1983, pl.20

70 Thomas, 1992, 205

71 Thomas, 1992, 204

72 Thomas, 1992, 179

73 Smiles & Pidgley, 1995, 89, 92, 102-4

74 Black, 1864, 257-8

75 Barber, 1981, 4-5

76 Harris, 1999, 53-56

77 Parkhouse, 2003a; 2003b

78 Thomas, 1992, 204

79 Rowe, 1848, 158-9

80 Hughes, 1857, 172

81 Fletcher, 1999; Owens, M., 1994

82 Greeves, 2004; Greenstreet, 1994

83 Evans, 1846, 105-109

84 Brown, 1999, 9, 1

85 medlibrary.org/medwik/RP Collier; Mobbs, n.d., 5-7

86 Murray, 1872, 228

87 Woodcock, 2008, 66

88 Cherry & Pevsner, 1989, 784

89 Vanstone, 1914, 4

90 Hughes, 1857, 644

91 Kelly, 1866, 1006

92 White, 1878-9, 762

93 Cherry & Pevsner, 1989, 781-2

94 Vanstone, 1914, 1

95 Hamilton Jenkin, 1974, 67

96 Woodcock, 1997, 25; 2008, 40

97 Brayshay, 1982, 119

98 Evans, 1846, 37

99 Radford, 1890

100 Plymouth Local Studies Library/Merrifield Collection

101 Hamilton Jenkin, 1974, 67-9

102 Woodcock, 1987

103 Woodcock, 1987

104 pers. comm. Virginia Noonan

105 Smiles & Pidgley, 1995, 111

106 Britton & Brayley, 1832, 8

107 *Exeter & Plymouth Gazette*, 21 August 1874

108 *Exeter & Plymouth Gazette*, 21 August 1874

109 *Western Times*, 19 September 1879

110 cf. Born, 1991, 226

111 Smiles & Pidgley, 1995; Le Messurier, 2002

112 Greeves, 2004, 87

113 Radford & Radford, 2000, 49

114 Smiles & Pidgley, 1995, 89-90

115 National Monuments Record neg.BB70/1577

116 Chugg, 1975, Pl.4

117 Talbot, 1846

118 Hughes, 1857

119 Hughes, 1857, Additions and Alterations

120 *Exeter Flying Post*, 19 April 1855

121 *Exeter Flying Post*, 4 January 1855

122 *Exeter Flying Post*, 9 April 1857; 6 May 1858

123 Kelly, 1866, 1234-5

124 Kelly, 1883, 732

125 Payne, 2005

126 Scott, 1985, 22

127 Gordon, 2013, 27-8

128 Burnard, 1890-94

129 Martin, 2014, 5-6

130 *The London Gazette*, 7 March 1862, 1345; 18 April 1862, 2091

131 Fox, 1864

132 Thomas, 1988, 12-14

133 Thomas, 1988, 65

134 Thomas, 1988, 65-68

135 Scott, 1985, 50-51

136 pers. comm. Virginia Noonan

137 Woodcock, 1997, 10

138 Spreat, 1842; Bhanji, 2010, 220-221

139 Thomas, 1988, 22

140 Thomas, 1988, 22

141 Bhanji, 2010, 220

142 Greeves, 2012, 91

143 Scott, 1985, 58

144 Scott, 1985, 57-58

145 Thomas, 1988, 45

146 Thomas, 1988, 139-140

BIBLIOGRAPHY

Barber, T. (1981) *Recollections of Ivybridge and District*

Bedford, F. (1867) 'Landscape Photography and its Trials', *Yearbook of Photography and Photographic News Almanac*, 1867, 22-3

Bhanji, S. (2010) 'The Victorian carte de visite photograph: a neglected source of Devon's topographical history', *Trans. Devon. Assoc.*, 142, 209-236

Black, A. & C. (1864) *Black's Guide to Devonshire* (Edinburgh)

Born, A. (1991) 'Limestone, limekilns and the limeburning industry north and west of Dartmoor', *Trans. Devon. Assoc.*, 123, 213-240

Brayshay, M. (1982) 'The Duke of Bedford's Model Cottages in Tavistock 1840-1870', *Trans. Devon. Assoc.*, 114, 115-131

Britton, J. & Brayley, E. (1832) *Devonshire & Cornwall Illustrated* (London)

Brodie, A., Croom, J. & Davies, J. (2002) *English Prisons – An Architectural History* (English Heritage, Swindon)

Broughton, D. (1968/9) 'The Birch Tor & Vitifer Tin Mining Complex', *Trans. Cornish Institute of Engineers*, 24, 25-49, 50-53

Brown, M. (1999) *Dartmoor Field Guides*, 54 vols (privately published, Plymouth)

Burnard, R. (1890-1894) *Dartmoor Pictorial Records* (facsimile edn, 1986, Devon Books, Exeter)

Chapple, W. (1779) *Description and Exegesis of the Drew's Teignton Cromlech* (privately published)

Cherry, B. & Pevsner, N. (1989) *The Buildings of England – Devon* (Penguin Books, London)

Chugg, B. (1975) *Victorian and Edwardian Devon from Old Photographs* (Batsford, London)

Collier, R. (1849) *A Treatise on the Law Relating to Mines* (Benning, London)

Croker, J. (1852) *A Guide to the Eastern Escarpment of Dartmoor* (2nd edn, London)

Crossing, W. (1901) *A Hundred Years on Dartmoor* (Western Morning News, Plymouth)

Crossing, W. (1902) *The Ancient Stone Crosses of Dartmoor and its Borderland* (revised edn, Commin, Exeter)

Crossing, W. (1909) *Guide to Dartmoor* (Western Morning News, Plymouth)

Duprez, L. (1870) *Duprez's Trip up the Tamar* (Smith & Perry, Plymouth)

Evans, R. (1846) *Home Scenes or Tavistock and its Vicinity* (Simpkin & Marshall, London)

Fletcher, M. (1999) *The Ferro Ceramic Mine and Shaugh Brickworks, Meavy, Devon* (English Heritage Survey Report, National Monuments Record, Swindon)

Fox, S. (1864) *Kingsbridge Estuary with Rambles in the Neighbourhood* (Friend, Kingsbridge)

Friend, G. (1989) *Memories of Moretonhampstead* (Devon Books, Exeter)

Gordon, S. (2013) *Cairo to Constantinople – Francis Bedford's Photographs of the Middle East* (Royal Collections Trust)

Gosse, P. (1865) *Sea and Land* (London)

Gray, T. (2001) *Dartmoor Engraved* (The Mint Press, Exeter)

Gray, T. & Rowe, M., eds (1997) *Travels in Georgian Devon – The Illustrated Journals of the Reverend John Swete (1789-1800), Volume I* (Devon Books/Halsgrove, Tiverton)

Greenstreet, A. (1994) 'Disastrous Manoeuvres on Dartmoor', *Dartmoor Magazine*, 35, Summer 1994, 10-11

Greeves, T. (1986) *Tin Mines & Miners of Dartmoor – A Photographic Record* (Devon Books, Exeter)

Greeves, T. (1996) 'Tin Smelting in Devon in the 18th and 19th Centuries' in Newman, P. (ed.) *The Archaeology of Mining & Metallurgy in South-West Britain* (Peak District Mines Historical Society), 84-90

Greeves, T. (2004) *Images of England – Dartmoor* (Tempus Publishing)

Greeves, T. (2012) 'William Pengelly's Torquay – The Photographic Record c.1860- c.1870', *Trans. Devon. Assoc.*, 144, 87-118

Greeves, T. (2014) 'Owlacombe Tinwork in the 15th Century', *Dartmoor Tinworking Research Group Newsletter*, 46, May 2014, 15-16

Greeves, T. & Somers Cocks, J. (1983) *A Dartmoor Century 1883-1983: One Hundred Years of the Dartmoor Preservation Association* (DPA Publication No.8, Postbridge)

Greeves, T. & Stanbrook, E. (2004) *The Clapper Bridge, Postbridge, Dartmoor* (Quay Publications, Tavistock)

Halloran, J. (1996) ' A Gentleman's Travel Journal on Dartmoor in 1856' in Gray, T., ed., *Devon Documents* (Devon & Cornwall Notes & Queries, Tiverton), 93-97

Hamilton Jenkin, A. (1974) *Mines of Devon Volume 1: The Southern Area* (David & Charles, Newton Abbot)

Hardiman, B. and Mortimer, I. (n.d., c.2012) *A guide to the history and fabric of St Andrew's Church, Moretonhampstead*

Harris, C. (1999) *Stowford Paper Mill and the Industrial Heritage of the Erme Valley* (Halsgrove, Tiverton)

Harris, H. (1968) *Industrial Archaeology of Dartmoor* (David & Charles, Newton Abbot)

Harrison, Harrod & Co (1862) *Postal Directory & Gazetteer of Cornwall & Devon*

Hayter-Hames, J. (1981) *A History of Chagford* (Phillimore)

Hemery, E. (1983) *High Dartmoor – Land and People* (Robert Hale, London)

Hughes, J. (1857) *M. Billing's Directory and Gazetteer of the County of Devon...* (Birmingham)

Joy, R. (2002) *Dartmoor Prison – A Complete Illustrated History Volume 2: The Convict Prison 1850-Present Day* (Halsgrove, Tiverton)

Kelly (1866) *The Post Office Directory of Somerset and Devon with Bristol* (London)

Kelly (1883) *Directory of Devonshire* (London)

Le Messurier, B. (2002) *Dartmoor Artists* (Halsgrove, Tiverton)

Lewis, F. (1821) *Scenery of the River Dart, being a series of Thirty-five views* (London)

Lysons, D. & S. (1822) *Magna Britannia – Volume the Sixth, containing Devonshire* (London)

Martin, A. (2014) *Viewing the Past: The Photographic Heritage of the Isles of Scilly* (Isles of Scilly Museum)

Matthew, A. (2010) 'Photography as Art and Social History Part I:The Francis Bedford Topographical Photographs from Birmingham Central Library', www.adam-matthew-publications.co.uk/collections_az/photos-1/description.aspx

Mildren, J. (1984) *Dartmoor in the Old Days* (Bossinney Books, Bodmin)

Mobbs, A. M. (n.d.) *Horrabridge and District, Part Four – Notable Local Families – The Colliers*

Murray, J. (1872) *A Handbook for Travellers in Devon & Cornwall* (8th edn revised)

Newman, P. (2002) *Headland Warren and the Birch Tor and Vitifer Tin Mines* (English Heritage, Archaeological Investigation Report Series A1/34/2002)

Ormerod, G. (1871) 'The Fall and Restoration of the Cromlech at Drewsteignton, in the County of Devon, 1862', *Trans. Devon. Assoc.*, 4 Pt.2, 409-411

Ormerod, G. (1872) 'Notice of the Fall and Restoration of "The Spinster's Rock", or Cromlech in the Parish of Drewsteignton, in the County of Devon, and of Stone Circles and Avenues formerly existing in the Vicinity', *The Archaeological Journal...of the Royal Archaeological Institute*, 29, 345-350 + figs

Ormerod, G. (1876) 'Historical Sketch of the Parish of Chagford', *Trans. Devon. Assoc.*, 8, 62-81

Owens, M. (1994) 'Industries Beneath Dewer, Part One', *Dartmoor Magazine*, 35, Summer 1994, 16-18

Parkhouse, N. (2003a) 'Broad-Gauge Bonus – Ivybridge', *Archive*, 39, September 2003, 37-39

Parkhouse, N. (2003b) 'Broad-Gauge Bonus – Replacing Brunel's South Devon Viaducts', *Archive*, 40, December 2003, 49-52

Payne, B. (2005) 'Brett Payne's Victorian & Edwardian Portrait Photo Collection' freepages.genealogy.rootsweb.ancestry.com/~brett/phot2/oangel.html

Polwhele, R. (1793) *Historical Views of Devonshire* (Exeter)

Proctor, M., Spooner, G. & Spooner, M. (1980) 'Changes in Wistman's Wood, Dartmoor: Photographic and other Evidence', *Trans. Devon. Assoc.*, 112, 43-79

Radford, G. H. (1890) 'Lady Howard of Fitzford', *Trans. Devon. Assoc.*, 22, 66-110

Radford, R. & U. (2000) *South Tawton & South Zeal with Sticklepath – A Thousand Years Beneath the Beacon* (Halsgrove, Tiverton)

Ravenhill, W., ed. (1965) *Benjamin Donn – A Map of the County of Devon 1765* (Devon & Cornwall Record Soc and Univ of Exeter)

Risdon, T. (1811 edn) [c.1630] *The Chorographical Description or Survey of the County of Devon* (London)

Rowe, S. (1830) 'Antiquarian Investigations in the Forest of Dartmoor, Devon; by Samuel Rowe, B.A. Member of the Plymouth Institution', *Transactions of the Plymouth Institution*, [Vol.1], 181-212

Rowe, S. (1848) *A Perambulation of the Antient and Royal Forest of Dartmoor and the Venville Precincts* (Plymouth)

Scott, C. G. (1985) 'Photographers in Devon 1842-1939 (a brief directory for photograph collectors)', *The Photo Historian Supplement no.101*

Smiles, S. & Pidgley, M. (1995) *The Perfection of England – Artist Visitors to Devon c. 1750-1870* (Univ of Plymouth)

Spencer, S. (2011) *Francis Bedford, Landscape Photography and Nineteenth-Century British Culture – The Artist as Entrepreneur* (Ashgate Publishing Ltd, Farnham)

Spreat, W. (1842) *Picturesque Sketches of the Churches of Devon drawn from nature and on stone* (Exeter)

Stanbrook, E. (1990), 'Fingle Mill – The Ruins Among the Trees', *Dartmoor Magazine*, 21, Winter 1990, 24-5

Sumner, I. (2010) *In Search of the Picturesque – The English Photographs of JWG Gutch 1856/59* (Westcliffe Books, Bristol)

Swete, J. [N.E.] (1796) 'On some of the more remarkable British Monuments in Devon' in *Essays by a Society of Gentlemen at Exeter* (Trewman & Sons, Exeter)

Talbot, W. H. F. (1846) in *The Art-Union*, Vol.8, June 1846, p.143.

Thomas, C. (1988) *Views and Likenesses – Early Photographers and their work in Cornwall and the Isles of Scilly 1839-1870* (Royal Institution of Cornwall, Truro)

Thomas, D. (1992) 'The Chronology of Devon's Bridges', *Trans. Devon. Assoc.*, 124, 175-206

Trollope, A. (1858) *The Three Clerks* (1907 edn, The World's Classics, Oxford University Press)

Vanstone, T. (1914) *Reminiscences of Places and Incidents in the Town of Tavistock in the Forties of the Nineteenth Century* (Tavistock Gazette)

Warner, R. (1800) *A Walk Through the Western Counties of England*

White, William (1878-9) *History, Gazetteer and Directory of the County of Devon* (Sheffield)

Woodcock, G. (1987) 'Turnpike Days', *Tavistock's Yesterdays - Episodes from Her History*, 3, 17-36

Woodcock, G. (1997) *Tavistock* (Chalford, Stroud).

Woodcock, G. (2008) *Tavistock – A History* (Phillimore, Chichester)

INDEX